Devotions
for the
Overwhelmed

Devotions for the Overwhelmed

MELODY CARLSON

CrossAmerica Books

CROSSINGS BOOK CLUB, GARDEN CITY, NEW YORK

CrossAmerica Books is an imprint and trademark
pending on behalf of Crossings Book Club.

Scripture quotations used in this book are from the Holy Bible,
New International Version®, copyright © 1973, 1978, 1984 by
International Bible Society, used by permission of Zondervan
Publishing House, all rights reserved; and from the New Revised
Standard Version Bible, copyright © 1989 by the Division of
Christian Education of the National Council of the Churches of
Christ in the USA, used by permission, all rights reserved.

Cover design by Sherry Sumerlin
Interior design by Debbie Glasserman

ISBN: 0-7394-2926-4

Printed in the United States of America

Devotions for the Overwhelmed

Take a Deep Breath

Come to me, all you who are weary and burdened,
and I will give you rest.

—Matthew 11:28

Another day, and you're running fast—racing the clock! You toss in a load of wash, drop off the kids, pick up the dry cleaning, and still make it to work on time—just barely. You conquer some giants at work (although some are still dogging your heels) and you rush through the rest of your day, fighting to get everything done. Finally, it's time to go home, but you feel like you've barely made a dent in your to-do list.

And did you even take a moment to breathe?

Life's demands seem to press from all angles, and we can become so caught up in the rat race that we almost forget the most fundamental elements of living—things like breathing deeply, relaxing, and simply enjoying the beauty God has placed all around us.

FOR FURTHER REFLECTION

Remember to pause during your busy day. Then take in a few deep breaths. Appreciate the soothing feeling of your lungs expanding with fresh air, as well as the calming effect of slowly exhaling.

PRAYER

Dear God, help me to remember the joy of simply breathing deeply. Increase my gratitude for the many ways You meet all my most basic needs. Amen

Love Yourself

Love your neighbor as yourself.

—Luke 10:27

Many times when we find ourselves overwhelmed, we rationalize and make good excuses, telling ourselves that we're harried like this because we're trying to serve others (important people like spouses, bosses, kids . . .). We convince ourselves that our cause is noble and worthwhile and beneficial. But we push ourselves far beyond our limits (we may not even realize our limits), as we agree to chair the PTA fundraiser, or allow ourselves to be bullied into taking someone else's shift in the carpool, or promise to water our neighbor's prized petunias, and in so doing we invite all forms of stress and pressure into our lives.

We may think we are motivated by love and commitment to others, but what we fail to see is that *we are not loving ourselves*. And when we neglect to love ourselves, everyone pays the price. For only as we love and honor our own lives can we truly love and honor those around us.

FOR FURTHER REFLECTION

Look into the mirror this morning and say, "God loves you and so do I." And as you move throughout your day, remember those precious words and make choices that reflect the love you have verbally expressed. Do this daily, determining to think more lovingly toward yourself.

PRAYER

*Dear Lord, help me to realize the wisdom
of Your words about loving my neighbor as myself.
Teach me to love myself with honesty and humility. Amen*

What Do You Really Want?

May he grant you your heart's desire, and fulfill all your plans.
—Psalm 20:4

When was the last time you really considered what it is you *want* out of life? And who, you may be wondering, has time for such philosophical frivolities anyway? Or perhaps you're afraid if you stopped to consider these things, you might only become more discouraged. But how can you begin to battle against the things that overwhelm you if you're unsure of what it is you truly desire? Do you long for peace? Then you must fight against confusion. Do you crave contentment? Then you must wage a campaign against everything that distracts you from that end.

For we cannot advance toward a goal we've never acknowledged. Without recognizing what it is we truly want, our chances of attaining it are slim. But as we realize and admit what's important to us, we can make a conscious plan to get there. And, as with all journeys, ours will begin with one small step.

FOR FURTHER REFLECTION

Ask yourself what it is you truly want out of this life. Be willing to quiet your heart to listen. And prepare yourself to receive whatever the answer may be. Then lay these things before God and ask Him to bless and lead you forward.

PRAYER

Creator of heaven and earth, show me what it is You've made me for. Help me to thoughtfully consider how I really want to live my life. Lead me in the way I should go to achieve it. Amen

Spinning Faster, Going Under

Yet when I surveyed all that my hands had done
and what I had toiled to achieve, everything was meaningless,
a chasing after the wind; nothing was gained under the sun.
—Ecclesiastes 2:11

Remember the old poster adage: "The faster I go, the behinder I get"? Doesn't it sometimes seem that as we accomplish more, or get jobs done more quickly, more (and often bigger) challenges begin to pile up before our very eyes? Perhaps it's because we take on too much, or are afraid to say "no." Or by performing so well, we send the message that we're able to do more—much, much more.

And before we realize what's happened, the merry-go-round of life is spinning faster and faster, and we don't have a clue as to how to get off. But we're not trapped. All we have to do is say "stop!" and hop off the merry-go-round and wait for the dizziness to pass. Then we can regroup and ask ourselves if this is how we really want to live.

FOR FURTHER REFLECTION

Honestly evaluate the pace of your life. Is this the speed you feel comfortable with? Do you long to slow things down? Are you willing to let some things go in order to improve the quality of your life? Consider one activity that you could eliminate and never miss.

PRAYER

Eternal God, help me to see myself as I truly am.
Reveal the areas of my life that are spinning out of control.
Show me if it's time to slow down. Amen

A Real Desire for Change

For he satisfies the thirsty and fills the hungry with good things.
—Psalm 107:9

Sometimes the very idea of change makes us uncomfortable. We get used to the status quo and think continuing along the same line might simply be easier. Sure, it might be a rut, but at least it's *our* rut and we know what to expect. But easier isn't always better—we know that in our hearts. And perhaps we've come to long for something better, more meaningful, more fulfilling in our lives.

And that's when we develop a real hunger for change. Yet, even as this desire starts growing within us, we're not always sure which direction to take. And, of course, we aren't looking for change for the sake of change—we just want something more satisfying to our souls. Perhaps we want a simpler way of living, or more time to pursue what's important to us, or just to more thoroughly enjoy the people we love. And to attain these rewards, we must embrace change.

FOR FURTHER REFLECTION

Imagine ways your life could be different. Start with something small. For instance, you might choose to give up some TV time for a quiet moment. Whatever it is, just play with this idea in your mind. Envision what it might be like to deliberately make a change.

PRAYER

Please, God, increase my openness toward change.
Help me to start small, and give me clarity and discernment
to know how I should proceed. Amen

An Honest Look at Your Life

He reveals deep and hidden things; he knows what lies
in darkness, and light dwells with him.
—Daniel 2:22

In reading this book, you are making a conscious effort to take stock of the way you live your life. And it's not an easy thing to do. In fact, other than when we make those idealistic New Year's resolutions that are quickly forgotten, most of us don't usually pause to look.

But what if we stepped back and took a good, long, hard look at where we've been and where we're going? What if we honestly attempted to account for the way we spend our days? What would we see? Surely, many fine and valuable things: the way we do our work, the way we help others, the way we love those around us. But we'd probably see a lot of other things, too. Maybe we wouldn't even be brave enough to look for long. But perhaps we could endure a short but candid glimpse.

FOR FURTHER REFLECTION

Try to watch how you live your life today. You might even jot down the activities that fill your day, and how they make you feel—fulfilled, stressed, happy, worried? For only as you observe what's really going on can you address ways you might want to change. Be brave, be honest, be willing to see what's really there.

PRAYER

Merciful God, I know You can see me, but sometimes it's as if I can't see myself. For just a moment, help me to see what You see—the successes as well as the challenges. Amen

Caught by the Storm

The ship was caught by the storm and could not head into the wind; so we gave way to it and were driven along.

—Acts 27:15

Have you ever noticed that it's the busiest people who are most willing to volunteer when help is needed? Perhaps it's because they're fairly organized, and feel confident and competent about adding more to their already-full schedules. Or maybe they feel they have a reputation to maintain. Perhaps they simply have difficulty saying "no."

We can be so concerned about not disappointing others that we put additional stresses into our own lives, just to keep from letting others down. Some people call us overachievers, but maybe we're just overcommitted. And maybe, if the truth were known, we'd discover that we're actually *under*achievers. Because, too often, when we're overextended, we're caught in a flurry of activity, accomplishing very little. Someone usually winds up suffering as a result, and it's almost always us (although we may gather up others in our storm, too).

FOR FURTHER REFLECTION

Think about whether or not you're overcommitted. Can you pinpoint a certain area of concern? Even if that part of your life may seem to be going well, is another part suffering as a result? Consider ways you can un-commit yourself. Then practice saying "no."

PRAYER

Lord, as much as I want to help everyone, I realize I can't agree to do everything. Please help me to know when and how to say "yes" as well as "no." Amen

Can You Hear Your Heart?

He stilled the storm to a whisper;
the waves of the sea were hushed.

—Psalm 107:29

Life can seem awfully noisy sometimes. Overwhelmingly so. Whether at work, or at home, it seems there is always someone speaking, someone asking something of us. Even the telemarketers hardly give us a moment's peace. And sometimes in this cacophony of life's noises, we forget how to tune in to our very own hearts. We forget how easily that quiet little voice inside us can be drowned out by those who speak more loudly. And yet, perhaps, the softest voice is the one we most need to listen to.

For only as we reconnect to our hearts and our spirits can we learn what we truly need—and what we don't. It is so easy to go day after day without hearing, but, oh, the sweet rewards when we tune in and listen!

FOR FURTHER REFLECTION

Find someplace away from the hubbub of life—even a closet will do. Now, take a few minutes to breathe deeply, quiet your thoughts, and relax. Then listen—listen to your heart. See if you can hear what your heart is saying to you. Remember this skill takes practice.

PRAYER

Father in heaven, I know You speak to hearts. And I know You have hidden some truths in mine. Please teach me to tune in. Help me to listen. I want to hear Your voice. Amen

Your Mission Statement

Go in peace. The mission you are on is under the eye of the Lord.
—Judges 18:6

If you've ever worked for a corporation, large or small, you've probably seen a mission statement before. A mission statement usually consists of several tightly focused sentences outlining objectives that are meant to espouse whatever goals are most important to that particular business. It's a way for a business to keep itself on target; to discern new directions; and to decline distracting opportunities that don't align with where the business is heading.

But what about your life? Surely, it's more important than a business. So, how does one go about creating a mission statement for life? And even if you could put your life goals down into words, how could you be sure they were right? Begin with a draft; it allows you the freedom to make alterations later, as needed.

FOR FURTHER REFLECTION

Begin to list the goals that are most important to you. Then prioritize these goals and try to word them into three to five simple sentences. Now, place your first draft mission statement where you can see it—every day. But remember, it's not written in stone; it's evolving, just like you.

PRAYER

God my Creator, I seek Your direction and guidance as I attempt to put order in my life. I realize that my plans and goals are worthless without Your continued blessing on them. Amen

From All Sides

No, in all these things we are more than conquerors through him who loved us.

—Romans 8:37

Some days it feels as if you're being pushed and pressed from every possible angle. And if you're not being pushed, then surely you're being stretched. And sometimes it can get downright uncomfortable. But what if there's nothing you can do about it?

While there are times when there is absolutely nothing we can do to change the *external* circumstances in our lives—accidents happen, appointments are cancelled, deadlines are moved up—there is still something we can do to control our *internal* circumstances.

We have an internal source of power. We can call upon God to give us the strength, the energy, the compassion—whatever it is we need to make it through. And knowing we have this resource available helps us to regain our sense of control and to maintain our composure.

FOR FURTHER REFLECTION

Decide now that no matter what stress comes your way today (and most likely some will!), you will call upon God to help you through. Remember that God has infinite stores of patience, love, compassion, peace, endurance, forgiveness . . . whatever it is you need.

PRAYER

Ever-present God, remind me to call upon You when I feel pressed in from all sides. Help me to see this as a reminder of how much I need Your help to succeed at living. Amen

Taking Baby Steps

Your beginnings will seem humble, so prosperous
will your future be.

—Job 8:7

One of the greatest challenges of overcoming a feeling of being overwhelmed is to remember that "Rome wasn't built in a day." In other words, we need to learn to rejoice over small victories and delight over baby steps. For each new step, no matter how small, moves us closer to where we want to be.

What parents are ever dismayed over their child's first steps? What mother would ever say, "Hey, that wasn't very good. Surely, you can take a bigger step than that?" Even when the baby stumbles and falls down, no loving parent scowls and says, "That sure was stupid, Junior." So, let's cut ourselves some slack here. And let's congratulate ourselves for each small step, and look forward to many more!

FOR FURTHER REFLECTION

Be aware of small areas where you are making progress. Have you let go of a stressful commitment? Have you said "no" lately? Have you been allowing yourself a ten-minute walk every day to clear your head and calm your nerves? Do you feel stress is just a tiny bit diminished? Even if only for a moment? Rejoice in these things!

PRAYER

Lord Jesus, help me to remember how much a parent rejoices as a child takes those first precious steps. Remind me that You take the same kind of joy in me. Amen

Make It Plain

Then the Lord answered me and said: Write the vision;
make it plain on tablets, so that a runner may read it.
                                              —Habakkuk 2:2

Sure, while under pressure, we may think we don't have time to
make lists, but a good list can help keep us on track. Making a list
can actually free us from hanging on to the insignificant details
that are cluttering up our minds. Making a list forces us to focus
on the tasks in front of us and to prioritize them. It can be a
tremendous relief to see in print—plain as day—that some of the
huge burdens we imagine looming over us don't actually need to
be dealt with immediately. Putting it all down on paper can clarify
what must be done and can help us set the order in which those
things get done, giving us a sense of control over our many tasks.

On the other hand, we must take care to be realistic in our list
making. We are not super-powered, so let's make lists that are
logical and sensible. And let's be willing to cross some things off
our lists.

FOR FURTHER REFLECTION

Practice making a daily to-do list. But be realistic. Can you really
run twelve errands on your lunch hour? What must *be done today?*
What can wait until tomorrow? Make sure you list a moment for
yourself—otherwise you might not get it!

PRAYER

God of love, teach me to use simple tools that will allow me to live
more freely. Help me to order my day so that I might avoid a
feeling of chaos and stress. Amen

The Buddy System

*A friend loves at all times, and kinsfolk
are born to share adversity.*

—Proverbs 17:17

Trying to overcome an area of weakness in your life can be a lonely struggle. But God did not intend for us to be solitary creatures. He knew we'd need others to help us along the way, to encourage us when we want to give up, and to lend a hand when we stumble.

Now, if we look around, surely we'll notice a friend who's struggling with stress and pressure, perhaps feeling she's about to go under. After all, stress has become almost a national epidemic (especially for working moms!). So let's see if there isn't someone else—someone we can relate to—who might like to team up to fight stress together. Who knows, we might find so many equally frazzled people that we'll want to start a club!

FOR FURTHER REFLECTION

Approach someone who you think would be a good buddy for you. Explain that you're trying to regain some control over the chaos in your life and invite him or her to consider joining you.

PRAYER

Precious Lord, I know You don't want us to live in isolation. We all need each other. Please, show me a friend to partner with—someone I can encourage and be encouraged by. Amen

Sharing the Wealth

You will surely wear yourself out, both you and these people
with you. For the task is too heavy for you;
you cannot do it alone.

—Exodus 18:18

Those of us with the tendency to become overwhelmed often have a number of characteristics in common. One of those is the way we frequently attempt to do everything ourselves. Sometimes it's because we actually think we can do it better than others. Or it's simply because we don't want to bother someone else by asking them for help. And occasionally we're afraid to ask, or think it's a waste of time because it's easier to do the job ourselves than to teach someone else how to do it.

But what we neglect to see is that not only do we need other people to help us, sometimes other people need *us* to let them help. When we play the "little red hen" and attempt to "do it all" we often rob others of the joy of getting involved. We need to learn how to delegate—to assign tasks and invite others to join in. And the better we become at this, the happier we'll all be!

FOR FURTHER REFLECTION

Think about the areas of your life where you're feeling overwhelmed by demands—at work or at home. Then consider who is less busy than you; who might be able to lighten your load. Next, plan how you will approach them. Be gracious but firm. And expect help—it may be exactly what someone is hoping to give.

PRAYER

Please, God, help me to realize that it's okay to ask for help.
Help me to see this not as a sign of weakness,
but an opportunity that allows someone else to share. Amen

Getting Unplugged

He makes me lie down in green pastures;
he leads me beside still waters; he restores my soul.
—Psalm 23:2, 3

Two hundred years ago, people had far more to do to keep themselves alive and well than we do today. They were often responsible for growing their own food, making their own clothes, doing laundry in a tub, splitting firewood—all sorts of demanding chores necessary just to survive. And yet they handled those responsibilities with a whole lot less stress than we seem to exhibit today—perhaps because they weren't bogged down with telephones, fax machines, and e-mail!

Sometimes we need to *unplug*—to disconnect ourselves from all the electronic demands of living in the twenty-first century. Maybe it's not quite as simple as turning off the TV and taking the phone off the hook, but all of us would do well to realize that we can actually survive for an hour, perhaps even a day!, without being electronically connected to the rest of the "civilized" world.

FOR FURTHER REFLECTION

Try to find a few minutes to completely "disconnect" from the rest of the world. Take a walk without your cell phone, beeper, and CD player. Turn off the TV, radio, and phone in your home. Whatever it takes, embrace peace in your life, and resolve to do so regularly.

PRAYER

Gracious Father, I know you are a God of peace.
And, truly, I long for peace. Please, show me practical ways I can incorporate the still waters into my daily living. Amen

The Need to Impress

You aren't swayed by men, because you pay no attention to who
they are; but you teach the way of God in accordance
with the truth.

—Mark 12:14

Another trait those of us who are overwhelmed tend to share
(although it's hard to admit it aloud) is that we often feel the need
to make a good impression. Perhaps we think it's for a worthwhile
reason—we want to set an example; we need to be a leader in the
workplace; we want our neighbors to respect us. Whatever our
rationale, we feel a strong need to impress. This need can hold
us hostage.

That's because we'll *never be able to do or be enough* to impress
everyone. There'll always be someone who won't fully appreciate
us. But we need to learn not to care. We need to stop worrying
about what others think and instead focus on what's right for us,
and those closest to us. With this acceptance comes great freedom.
We don't stop caring about other people, we just learn to suppress
our unhealthy need to impress them.

FOR FURTHER REFLECTION

Ask yourself if you've allowed what other people think to become too
important to you. Do you tend to perform for acceptance? Consider
how much stress this can add to your life. Think of one thing you
can do to stop going in this direction. Then do it.

PRAYER

Dear God, I know that You're the only one on whom I should be
trying to make an impression. And yet, all You ask of me is my
love and obedience. Let me live in a way that pleases You. Amen

Let It Out

Weeping may linger for the night,
but joy comes with the morning.

—Psalm 30:5

In addition to all of the physically draining demands we face, there are times when we are *emotionally* overloaded. Whether it be with sorrow or happiness—being emotionally overwhelmed can be a good thing. It's a natural way for us to cleanse ourselves of negative feelings and to fortify ourselves with positive ones.

Unfortunately, in our American culture we often seem to hold back from displaying our deepest emotions. Perhaps we stifle our feelings, afraid they're not socially acceptable. We could learn a thing or two from cultures that practice emotional freedom. Crying openly and passionately can alleviate stress. Laughing with hilarity and abandon can make us feel good. Let's learn to welcome these types of overwhelming feelings.

FOR FURTHER REFLECTION

Give yourself permission to feel things deeply, passionately, and with more freedom. Acknowledge that suppressed feelings can be harmful to your body and spirit. Let yourself cry when you need to, and allow yourself the joy of a good, long, healthy laugh.

PRAYER

God our Creator, You have made us with a full range of emotions. Please, help me to be aware of my feelings and show me ways to express them healthfully. Amen

Performers Anonymous

Look to the Lord and his strength;
seek his face always.

—1 Chronicles 16:11

We've already addressed our need to impress, but with many who are overwhelmed it goes further than that. There are those of us who have the need to *perform*. We find ourselves going far beyond what's expected—in essence we do "back-flips" for those around us. And that can really add stress to our lives.

But how do we escape this destructive cycle? If we recognize that it's a problem for us, we can ask ourselves why we do it. Are we looking for affirmation, attention, approval? If so, why are we looking to others to provide it? We need to remind ourselves that God loves us, and appreciates us, and understands us, and if we allow Him to, He'll give us all the affirmation we need. Giving the performance of our lives for an unresponsive audience will only serve to wear us out and irritate them, so let's remember who our biggest fan is and focus our efforts in His direction. When we stop doing "back-flips" for everyone else we receive the gifts of peace and acceptance in return.

FOR FURTHER REFLECTION

Ask yourself if you're ever a "performer." If so, then ask yourself if you're ready to change. Make a commitment to look to God for all the attention, approval, and applause that you're seeking from others.

PRAYER

Loving Father, help me to see myself as I truly am, and to know that You love me despite all that. Teach me how to live, not for the applause of others, but to please You. Amen

Admissions of Truth

And we, who with unveiled faces all reflect the Lord's glory,
are being transformed into his likeness with ever-increasing glory,
which comes from the Lord, who is the Spirit.

—2 Corinthians 3:18

It's not always easy to accept everything we see when we look at ourselves in the mirror. Perhaps it's because we're not seeing ourselves as we truly are. Maybe we're focusing on overblown flaws, magnified insecurities, and imagined imperfections. Is it possible our true image is hidden behind a veil of negative misconceptions? Of course we're not perfect, but we're probably doing a whole lot better than we usually admit.

So, let's take another look. But first let's remove the veil and try to see ourselves as God, the One who created us, might. And before we do this, let's consider the way a parent looks at their beloved child. Perhaps it is through rose-colored glasses—or maybe it's only that love sees things in a whole different light. As we look into our lives through our loving Father's eyes, let's be candid and honest.

FOR FURTHER REFLECTION

Sit down with a pad and pencil and list as many of your positive attributes as you can. Be honest (no one but you will see this list). Write down everything that pops into your mind, whether you believe it or not. Then study the list and think about what you've discovered.

PRAYER

Almighty God, help me to see myself the way You see me.
Help me to acknowledge all the gifts and potential You've so
graciously planted inside me. Amen

Serenity

*Surely then you will find delight in the Almighty and will lift up
your face to God. You will pray to him, and he will hear you,
and you will fulfill your vows.*

—Job 22:26, 27

Being continually overwhelmed can become something of an addiction in itself. You can call it being obsessive-compulsive or codependent, or even having an adrenaline addiction. But no matter the label, it's never healthy. And since many people dealing with addiction have found comfort in the Serenity Prayer, let's consider incorporating it into our prayer lives as well:

*God, grant me the serenity to accept
the things I cannot change, courage to
change the things I can, and wisdom
to know the difference. Amen*

FOR FURTHER REFLECTION

Write down this simple little prayer and post it someplace where you will see it throughout the day (like the refrigerator or your computer). Memorize it, and then begin to pray it with sincerity, actually considering the meaning of each word.

PRAYER

Lord, I know You don't need me to call out to you in formulated prayers. But sometimes I might need to. Help me to understand the full meaning of those transforming words. Amen

Taking Control

But the fruit of the Spirit is love, joy, peace, patience, kindness,
goodness, faithfulness, gentleness and self-control.
Against such things there is no law.

—Galatians 5:22, 23

One of the worst frustrations for someone who feels inundated and overwhelmed is the fear of losing control. But the desire to be in control is, in itself, often one of the main causes of our stress and anguish. Because some of us, whether we like to admit it or not, tend to be control freaks. We want everything running smoothly—and just the way we like it. And that alone can leave us feeling pretty overwhelmed.

But let's face it, the only thing we can really control in life is our own behavior. Everyone and everything else is out of our control. So, let's concentrate on taking charge of our own lives, our own decisions, our own goals. For once we recognize and accept the fact that we can't run the world we can focus our energy in more positive, fruitful, and God-inspired directions.

FOR FURTHER REFLECTION

Look at your own life; consider an area that may be "out of control."
Then ask yourself what you can do to regain control. Maybe it's changing the words you speak or the food you eat, or how you drive or how you react to certain aggravations. Choose one area, and then take control!

PRAYER

God of the universe, help me to be aware of areas where
I need to demonstrate self-control. Then show me how to do this.
And remind me to rejoice in any areas of victory. Amen

Divine Discernment

Trust in the Lord with all your heart and lean not on your own understanding; in all your ways acknowledge him, and he will make your paths straight.

—Proverbs 3:5, 6

Sometimes, especially when we're overwhelmed, it's tough to make good choices. So many tempting options can distract us from knowing what's really best for us. And often this can cause us to simply make no choices at all. We just wait and "let life take its course." Yet *failing* to make a clear choice is actually a decision within itself—and usually a decision that adds stress to our lives.

These are the times we need some divine discernment. We need to come to God and invite His guidance and direction into our lives. And to do so, we must entrust Him with everything we've got. We must believe that He really knows what's best for us.

FOR FURTHER REFLECTION

Is there a specific area of your life where you feel confused? Come quietly before God and place this area before Him. Ask for His help and guidance—and expect that He will give it. Maybe not today. But trust that He will show you.

PRAYER

Dear Lord, I admit that I need direction in my life. Please help me trust You completely so I can see the way You want me to go.
Amen

Just Say "No!"

*You are indeed my rock and my fortress; for your name's sake
lead me and guide me, take me out of the net
that is hidden for me, for you are my refuge.*

—Psalm 31:3, 4

"Just say no." Don't we hear this all the time? Like it's the one, surefire way for an overly busy person to avoid some additional stress in their life. And yet, why is it so hard to utter that simple two-letter word? Is it a fear of rejection? Or of hurting another? Do we feel that something will go completely undone or fall totally apart if we decline to participate? Are we afraid there's no one else able to do it? Or that someone else might do it better?

Perhaps we'll never know all the reasons we struggle with saying "no." And maybe it doesn't matter. Perhaps the most important thing is to simply develop the ability to say it. We don't need to give specific reasons (which might encourage someone to press us further), but we might want to practice a polite way to put it. "Thanks for asking, but I must decline," or "I appreciate you thinking of me, but I'm unable to participate" might be good ways to start.

FOR FURTHER REFLECTION

Consider whether there's something you need to say "no" to. If not, practice ways that you will say "no" the next time someone asks you to do something that's not in your best interest. Try taping a "Just say no" note near your telephone.

PRAYER

*Dear God, please help me to know when it's time to decline.
I realize I shouldn't say "no" to everything, but I know that I can't
do everything either. I need Your guidance. Amen*

Old Habits Can Be Broken

But in keeping with his promise we are looking forward to a new
heaven and a new earth, the home of righteousness. So then,
dear friends, since you are looking forward to this, make every
effort to be found spotless, blameless and at peace with him.
—2 Peter 3:13, 14

In today's culture it's almost impossible to live a life that's stress-free without choosing to make some specific changes. This usually entails breaking free from some old ways of thinking, and eliminating some unhealthy habits. Obviously, this isn't the same for everyone, but we usually know which habits add unnecessary stress to our lives.

Still, established patterns are hard to change. We get used to living a certain way. Even if a particular habit is killing us, it's hard to stop. Just ask any smoker. But the truth is, old habits can be broken if we've reached a place where we're ready to commit to change, and especially when we're willing to invite God's help. Many experts agree it takes two weeks to break a habit. So let's be patient, focus on only one habit, and then take it one day at a time.

FOR FURTHER REFLECTION

Acknowledge that you may have a habit that's unhealthy. It might be worrying, or procrastinating, or overcommitting. Maybe it's eating poorly or not allowing yourself time to unwind. Whatever it is, you must admit to it, and be willing to change.

PRAYER

Merciful Father, please, show me if there's something in my life that needs to be dealt with. Then help me to make the choice to change, and strengthen me to do it. Amen

The Law of Love

If I give all I possess to the poor and surrender my body
to the flames, but have not love, I gain nothing.

—1 Corinthians 13:3

If one single attribute could rule every area of our entire lives—oh, that it might be love. For if we were consistently governed by real, true love it would be nearly impossible to make bad choices. And it would be virtually impossible to feel overwhelmed because our energy and joy would never be depleted the way it is when we're doing something merely out of a sense of obligation or responsibility. As a result our lives would be fairly stress free and peaceful. *Heavenly.*

And so, if we could ever train our minds (and our hearts) to make every decision based on love for God, for others, and for ourselves, what a simple and effective measuring stick that would be. But it's never that easy, is it? Yet, it's something we could all consider and aspire toward. And, who knows, perhaps over time, and with God's help, we'll get better at it!

FOR FURTHER REFLECTION

Throughout your day, consider whether love is the motivation for your decisions and actions. Ask yourself: "Am I loving God by doing this right now?" Or: "Am I doing this because I love so-and-so?" Or: "Is this a loving thing to do to myself?" If anything else is your motivating factor your efforts will probably be in vain.

PRAYER

Kind Creator, I really do long to be ruled by love. But it seems so hard sometimes. My human nature likes to get in the way. Please help me and show me how I can improve. Amen

Filtering Out

Finally, beloved, whatever is true, whatever is honorable,
whatever is just, whatever is pure, whatever is pleasing,
whatever is commendable, if there is any excellence
and if there is anything worthy of praise,
think about these things.

—Philippians 4:8

Have you ever stopped to consider all the messages we take in throughout the course of a day? Some we hear audibly; some we simply perceive or imagine from the actions of others; some we actually say to ourselves. And many of these messages are positive and good. But, unfortunately, many are negative and harmful. And yet, how rarely we sift through these messages, tossing out the ones we really don't need to hear. In fact, we often replay—and dwell on—the negative ones.

But it's possible to make a conscious choice to filter out these negative messages. Of course, it takes practice and time—and we may have the most difficult time of all getting ourselves to stop making self-deprecating comments—but if we put our minds to it, we can learn to quickly recognize them, and then choose to cancel them out and forget about them. And this allows our minds greater opportunity to focus on the more wholesome messages.

FOR FURTHER REFLECTION

Pay attention to the messages you receive today (especially the ones you send yourself). Recognize those that say derogatory things like "that's stupid" or "you really blew that!" and try to cancel them out. Replace them with positive, uplifting messages that strengthen and inspire you.

PRAYER

Dear Jesus, show me the way to block out the negative things I hear about myself and replace those messages that undermine and destroy with Your messages of encouragement and love. Amen

Pause and Refresh

The Lord replied, "My Presence will go with you,
and I will give you rest."

—Exodus 33:14

Most people take a break at some point during their busy day (or at least would like to). In fact, there are employment laws stipulating that *all* workers *must* have regularly scheduled breaks. But too often, in the rush of things, we deny ourselves these needed respites. We just don't see how we can spare the time when our desks are stacked high or the list of errands and chores seems never-ending.

And, even when we do take breaks, we don't always allow ourselves to be truly refreshed—perhaps because we're still in overdrive and don't know how to decelerate. But we can learn to slow down and tune in to our souls; we can focus on what we need to do to stay healthy. Sometimes we might need a quiet break, just us and God. And sometimes we might need a short, brisk walk. Occasionally, we might need a nap or something cool to drink. But we need to pause and refresh ourselves—often. Because, the truth is, no one else can do it for us.

FOR FURTHER REFLECTION

Force yourself to take a break or two today. Tune into your mind, body, and spirit and see if you can figure out what sort of break might really refresh you. Then make it happen. You cannot deprive yourself of mental, physical, and spiritual refreshment; if you try to you will become completely depleted and then be of no use to anyone.

PRAYER

Dear God, help me to realize that ultimately, I must care for myself. Show me ways I can do it wisely. Help me to see the importance of refreshing myself regularly. Amen

The "P" Word

*And now what are you waiting for? Get up, be baptized and
wash your sins away, calling on his name.*

—Acts 22:16

Procrastination. It's *not* a very pretty word, is it? It smacks of
negativity and suggests slow starts, prolonged waits, unnecessary
delays, and unfinished tasks. And when we want something done
quickly, we rarely turn to a procrastinator for help. And yet it's
something we who are overwhelmed often turn to as a form of
escape. "I'll just do this later . . . I'll deal with this when I have
more time . . . Maybe it will just go away—I hope—because I
never have more time. . . ."

Yet, believe it or not, some forms of procrastination can be
good. Sometimes a slight delay allows us to contemplate a job and
mull over the best way to handle it. But the other form of
procrastination is debilitating. The work simply piles up and
eventually adds stress to our lives. That's when we need to jump in
and get things done. And that's when we realize it was only our
unfounded fear of the task that made us feel it was too big or too
hard in the first place.

FOR FURTHER REFLECTION

*Practice the "do it now" method. If something disagreeable or
challenging must be done, then get it done quickly and move on.
Don't overthink it or make it a bigger deal than it is. Post a "Just do
it!" note on your computer or refrigerator as a reminder that it's
usually best to jump in and get it over with.*

PRAYER

*Help me, God, to recognize the pitfalls of procrastination.
Show me ways I can avoid it and stay on top of things so I don't
overwhelm myself unnecessarily. Amen*

Be Thankful

And whatever you do, in word or deed, do everything in the name of Lord Jesus, giving thanks to God the Father through him.
—Colossians 3:17

Sometimes when we're battling difficult things like stress, fatigue, or being overwhelmed, we tend to focus on all the negatives. We see what's wrong with our lives, we give attention to all the areas that fall short. Yet this only leads us to deeper feelings of hopelessness, anxiety, and tension. And in a vicious cycle we dig ourselves deeper and deeper into the pit of despair.

And that's when it's time to stop, look around, and be thankful! It's time to take our eyes off the bad and redirect them to the good. To, in essence, count our blessings. For we quickly discover that as we embrace a grateful spirit and a thankful heart, the world suddenly looks a whole lot better.

FOR FURTHER REFLECTION

Take time to think about all the delightful blessings in your life. People you love, those who love you . . . the grass, the trees, the sky . . . animals, children, music, color . . . your health, your ability to see, hear, taste, smell . . . whatever it is that makes you happy.

PRAYER

Heavenly Father, I sincerely thank You for all You've given me. Help me to maintain this kind of focus. Teach me to live each and every day with a truly grateful heart. Amen

Not Enough Hours in the Day?

*And God blessed the seventh day and made it holy, because
on it he rested from all the work of creating that he had done.*
—Genesis 2:3

What if, suddenly, the number of hours in the day was flexible?
The fact is, we don't have to be ruled by the clock. We can adjust
our attitude toward time and make it work for us. We can create
a time budget not completely unlike the household budget we use
(or *ought* to use!). But unlike in the household budget, we can get
a little creative with the accounting in our time budget. What if
we imagined there were suddenly twenty-eight hours in each day?
Great, right? Now you'd actually have a shot at getting everything
done. Or would more responsibilities creep in and more tasks find
their way to you until, before you knew it, you were back to
running behind? Now imagine that there are only *twenty* hours in
the day. If you had to get everything done in that time, you'd make
it work, wouldn't you? So why not pretend the day is shorter and
put the extra hours into a time bank? Then you can make
withdrawals of time to nourish your soul. Just remember—this
time bank offers only "use it or lose it" accounts. If you don't
collect your "bonus" hours daily—their gone—forever.

FOR FURTHER REFLECTION

*Consider how you allow your workload to spread out to the number
of hours you think you have to do it. Try cutting back on the extra
hours you allot to your work or your chores. Just pretend there aren't
any more hours in the day to give to the work. And enjoy the
freedom of the extra hours you collect from the time bank.*

PRAYER

*Almighty God, help me to remember that You created the universe
and did so with time left over for a holy day of rest. Teach me to
plan my day wisely so that I no longer feel like I'm racing the clock.
Help me to make room in each day for restorative rest. Amen*

Wisdom for the Day

If any of you is lacking in wisdom, ask God, who gives to all generously and ungrudgingly, and it will be given you.
—James 1:5

Wouldn't you like to just wake up some morning and suddenly feel very wise? But wisdom usually doesn't happen like that. It's not an overnight process. On the other hand, scripture promises (over and over) that if we seek wisdom, we will find it. And, next to God, what better thing is there to seek than wisdom?

So what if we, who are trying not to be overwhelmed, decided to start each day asking God (the Father of all wisdom) to impart a small portion of His wisdom to us. Just enough for the day. Or what if we invited Him to lead and direct us throughout our entire day, saturated with His wisdom. Do you think the course of our lives would change? Do you think we'd be a little less overwhelmed? Would we feel better equipped to deal with those coming to us for answers? Only one way to find out!

FOR FURTHER REFLECTION

Come quietly before God and express your desire to learn from Him. Perhaps begin by asking for enough wisdom to get you through the day. Wait expectantly for His answer, and as you go out into the world to live your day, be on the lookout for the wisdom He is imparting all along the way.

PRAYER

Teach me, Lord, to come to You for real wisdom. Help me to hear, respect, and honor it. Show me how to use it in my daily life.
Amen

Attitude Adjustment

*But I tell you that men will have to give account on the day of
judgment for every careless word they have spoken.
For by your words you will be acquitted, and
by your words you will be condemned.*

—Matthew 12:36, 37

When someone you haven't seen for a while calls and asks how
you've been doing, do you often say something like: "Oh, I'm fine,
but I've been pretty busy lately"? So many of us give an answer to
this effect. We don't even think about it because it's almost
automatic. And, to be honest, it's perhaps quite descriptive of the
way we actually live or have been living. But if we're honestly
seeking to make changes and to slow things down, perhaps we
need to adjust the way we perceive ourselves and our lives. And
maybe we need to come up with a new answer besides "I've been
so busy."

For instance, we could say: "I'm learning to slow down and
really enjoy life." Now, wouldn't *that* raise some eyebrows. "Enjoy
life?" they might think. And perhaps they'd even inquire as to how
you reached this wondrous new place.

FOR FURTHER REFLECTION

*Try to rephrase some of the responses you so patently toss back to those
who ask. Think of ways to describe what it is you're actually trying
to accomplish in life. Change your attitude and see if it doesn't alter
your choices, actions, and even your language.*

PRAYER

*Dear God, help me to believe that my life is changing.
And help me to express these changes verbally.
Let me speak the truth in faith. Amen*

All We Desire

For where your treasure is, there your heart will be also.
                                                              —Luke 12:34

Our nation seems to have become consumed with consumerism. The average American feels the need to "have it all." And even if we're not completely sure what "having it all" means, we're relatively certain it means we need something more or something *else*. At least that's what all the advertisements—designed to make us feel discontent—want us to believe.

But do you actually know anyone who has "everything"? Or even if someone appears to, do you know that they are truly *happy* and contented? So why do we buy into such deceit? And do we ever stop to think about all the care and maintenance our possessions, gizmos, and gadgets need? And how much of our time and energy is lost forever in pursuit of these elusive tokens of success? Maybe the pitches sound so good that we just can't resist, but if we could put an end to this "having it all" dream, we might actually discover real happiness and contentment. Perhaps the happiest people you know are those who have already discovered that the simple and unfettered lifestyle has immeasurable rewards.

FOR FURTHER REFLECTION

Throughout the day, try to practice the art of contentment. Observe all that's around you that makes you happy and adds meaning to your life. Notice how little of it has to do with money or influence. Remember to thank God for simple pleasures.

PRAYER

Remind me, God, that I can only "have it all" when I am completely contented and happy with what You've given me. Thank you for taking such good care of me. Amen

Whose Life is This Anyway?

Trust in the Lord forever, for in the Lord God
you have an everlasting rock.

—Isaiah 26:4

Have you ever noticed how the more tightly we hold onto something, the more apt we are to lose it? Whether it's relationships with people, a position at work, or even a handful of sand; when we cling too tightly, too firmly, it tends to escape us. But what about our own lives? Can't we do as we wish with them? Or is it possible that we can grasp and clutch too tightly to them as well?

Yet, if we perceive our lives as gifts from God, perhaps we'll handle them with more care. Plus, if we're trusting God with our lives, we'll subsequently experience far less fear, anxiety, and stress. Because we begin to realize we're resting in God's hands. And although they are *our* lives and *our* choices as to how we live them, we will be able to relax knowing that He who made us also has His eye on us.

FOR FURTHER REFLECTION

Stop to consider who's really in control of your life. Is it you and you alone? Are you holding onto it with tightly clenched fingers? Or do you understand that your life is a gift from God and that He wishes to share and partake of it with you?

PRAYER

God my Creator, remind me that I truly do belong to You—
that You made me, and You have a special plan for me.
Help me to loosen my grasp and to trust You more. Amen

Living Better with Less

*Therefore I tell you, do not worry about your life, what you will eat
or drink; or about your body, what you will wear. Is not life more
important than food, and the body more important than clothes?*
—Matthew 6:25

There's an art to living in simple abundance. But we'll never
experience this beauty unless we deliberately slow down and realign
our priorities. Just like stopping to smell the roses—we have to
make the choice. Because if you rush right past, never diverting
your gaze to admire the roses' loveliness, never pausing to smell
their sweet fragrance, you'll miss out.

Are we missing out on life? If we spend too much time
commuting, perhaps we should seriously consider seeking a new
job closer to home. Or, even moving to be closer to work. We also
might want to think about moving if our houses are overwhelming
us. Are we sure we're living in the type of place best suited for us?
Or is the upkeep out of all proportion to the joy we experience
there? On a less radical front, perhaps we can wrangle leaving work
a little early every now and then, using the time to gather a bouquet
of posies to place with a lovingly prepared meal. Or to take an
evening stroll, pausing to look up at the sky. Or to hold a sleepy
child a moment longer, pausing to drink in her sweetness. So many
simple pleasures arise when we make the time to find them.

FOR FURTHER REFLECTION

*Watch for the simple pleasures that are dispersed throughout your
day. Determine to enjoy these moments, perhaps even jot them
down—what they are and how they make you feel. Commit yourself
to looking for more simple pleasures each day.*

PRAYER

*Dear Lord, help me to notice all the wonders you've placed around me.
Show me ways I can slow my life down in order to live it better. Amen*

Letting God Care for Us

But even if you do suffer for doing what is right, you are blessed.
—1 Peter 3:14

Most of us do not pass through life without caring for someone at some point in time. And many of us spend a great deal of time caring for others. But being a caregiver has its own sources of frustration and can be stressful and overwhelming. And, unfortunately, there can be stints when it seems there is no relief anywhere, and no end in sight. It's at these times we really need to allow God to care for us.

Because as much as we love those in our care, our well of compassion can go dry. And we may find ourselves moving through the actions of caring with hearts that are cold and hard. But if we can admit our weakness and call out to the One who cares for all, we will find relief and refreshment, and courage for the day. He may guide us to earthly resources where a temporary caregiver may be found to periodically spell us; He may lead us to just the right people at church who are searching for a way to help; He will certainly envelop us in His loving presence to renew our strength.

FOR FURTHER REFLECTION

If you feel overwhelmed by the care you give to those who depend on you, remind yourself that you need to depend on God. Allow God to care for you. Ask Him for love, strength, grace, patience—and perhaps an earthly source of relief in the form of a friend— whatever it is you need to make it through the day.

PRAYER

Merciful Father, sometimes I become overwhelmed when caring for others. Help me to honestly admit this to You, and come to You for the help and caring I need. Amen

Lightening the Load

Get rid of all bitterness, rage and anger, brawling and slander, along with every form of malice. Be kind and compassionate to one another, forgiving each other, just as in Christ God forgave you.
—Ephesians 4:31, 32

Who hasn't been hurt at some time in their life? It's just a natural result of the human condition. Whenever different personalities interact, especially under the crush of work deadlines; or during sensitive negotiations on a volunteer committee; or even from the highly charged sidelines of a soccer match, feelings can be hurt. But another natural part of our human condition is that an old hurt that's not forgiven can turn into a bitterness. And bitterness can rob us of energy and the daily joy of living. Not only that, but it can root into our lives and slowly poison our way of living and thinking. So, instead of being hurt once by someone, we end up reliving that hurt over and over and over again.

That's why we need to forgive and eliminate bitterness. But we cannot do it alone. Sure, we can consciously choose to change the way we think about someone who's hurt us, and we can forgive them. But only God can eradicate all traces of bitterness. We need to invite Him to do so. And then, having shed the overwhelming weight of bitter feelings, we can live freely and with joy!

FOR FURTHER REFLECTION

Examine your heart to see if you harbor bitterness toward someone. It could be a parent, a sibling, an old love, an ex, a neighbor—just about anyone. Honestly admit to yourself, and to God, that this is a problem for you. Choose to forgive and let it go. And ask God to help you.

PRAYER

Dear Jesus, please show me if I'm allowing bitterness to remain in my heart. Help me to do all I can to eradicate it, and then to trust You to do the rest. Thank You! Amen

Forgive Yourself as You Have Been Forgiven

If we confess our sins, he who is faithful and just will forgive us our sins and cleanse us from all unrighteousness.

—1 John 1:9

Sometimes it's actually easier to forgive others than it is to forgive ourselves. And often we don't even realize how much we *need* to forgive ourselves. But one sure signal that it's time to forgive ourselves is when we experience guilt—and guilt is overwhelming. When we have feelings of guilt (often for things that affect only ourselves), it's a red flag that we need to admit our mistakes and forgive ourselves. Then, hopefully, we can forget it, and move on. Carrying guilt around is like moving through life with a bag of rocks tied to your back. It depletes your energy and joy (and it *hurts*, for crying out loud!).

Of course, there are also those times when we've hurt others (whether intentionally or not) and we need to go directly to them, admit our error, and ask them to forgive us. But once again, we *still* need to forgive ourselves. And then move on!

FOR FURTHER REFLECTION

Think about whether you struggle with guilt. If so, consider the source and make the decision to deal with it. Go and apologize if necessary. But then forgive yourself. Look into the mirror and speak the words "I forgive you" aloud. As many times as it takes.

PRAYER

Dear God, I confess I've blown it. I know You've forgiven me. Please, help me to forgive myself and to learn from my mistakes. Give me a gracious and forgiving heart. Amen

Would Anything Be Left Unspoken?

But about that day or hour no one knows, neither the angels in heaven, nor the Son, but only the Father.

—Mark 13:32

When we listen to people who have survived a life-threatening situation we notice how their priorities and perspectives have changed. Suddenly, they're aware of what's really important—things like healing old relationships, telling someone dear that they love them, and really paying attention to the people around them. They recognize that every day might be their last, and become more determined than ever to live each day fully and well.

Wouldn't it be wonderful if we could all adapt that attitude? Since September 11th it would be hard to find anyone who hasn't thought very seriously about their priorities in life. That awful day brought thousands of stories of people whose priorities were straight. The messages they left were heartbreakingly simple: "I love you." Treating others (and ourselves) with the love and respect we'd give if we thought this was our last day on earth is an admirable way to live.

FOR FURTHER REFLECTION

As tragic events always remind us, we simply don't know when we will be called home. As you go through your day, interacting with various people, consider what you would say if you knew it would be your last encounter. Perhaps more importantly, what wouldn't you say? Oh, the pain and stress that might be avoided if we refrained from saying the things sometimes blurted out in the hectic haze of our days.

PRAYER

Eternal God, help me not to take these earthly days for granted. Who, besides You, knows how many I have? Help me to live each day as if it were my last, being guided by love above all. Amen

Remember the Child

*Truly I tell you, whoever does not receive the kingdom of God
as a little child will never enter it.*

—Luke 18:17

Deep inside each of us is a small child—a part of us that may be buried deep but has never gone away. A part of us who holds some of the keys to why we are who we are, and how we can become who we're meant to be. But in growing up and putting on adult ways and responsibilities, we may have repressed that child's voice or closed that child's eyes. Perhaps we had a painful childhood and have trouble revisiting that part of our past. But to be all we can be, we must allow that child to live.

For it is the child in us who takes delight in the simple pleasures of everyday life. It is the child who reminds us *it's time to play!* And the child who forces our gaze upwards to the starry heavens; and makes our eyes blink at the wonder of God's creation. So, let's tap into that small child again and rejoice in the glee of youth—youth as God always intended for every child.

FOR FURTHER REFLECTION

Search your memory for a particularly pleasant moment from your childhood. And as you remember, see if you can reconnect to the emotions you felt as a child. Then take those feelings with you throughout the day, applying them to your everyday world.

PRAYER

Father in heaven, You said we must become like children to enter Your kingdom. Please, help me to welcome again such childlike qualities as love, faith, and joy into my life. Amen

Where Are You Going?

Enter through the narrow gate; for the gate is wide and the road is easy that leads to destruction, and there are many who take it.
—Matthew 7:13

The busier people become the less they seem to notice where they're going. For instance, if we're dodging rush-hour traffic along a twelve-lane interstate, it's easy to miss the exit we'd actually meant to take. Isn't life like that too? The more caught up we get in the daily demands, the more we lose sight of where we originally thought we were headed.

The only answer seems to be to slow down and look around. To pause and take notice and remember *where* it is we actually want to be down the road—before we miss an important turn. Perhaps it's time to take another look at that "mission statement" that we're trying to create for our lives. Or perhaps it's time to come before the One who directs all traffic and ask for new or better directions. Whatever we do, we need to remember *where it is we're going*, if we really want to get there.

FOR FURTHER REFLECTION

Pause today to look, once again, at how you're spending your time and energy. Ask yourself if you're headed in the direction you truly intend to go. Of course, life often has unexpected detours, but it's up to us to keep ourselves on track.

PRAYER

God of the universe, remind me, once again, where I should be headed. Then help me to set my life in that direction.
For I know that only by Your help and grace can I arrive. Amen

Reinventing Yourself

*I am about to do a new thing; now it springs forth,
do you not perceive it? I will make a way in the wilderness
and rivers in the desert.*

—Isaiah 43:19

The thought of reinventing ourselves may sound silly or even impossible, but perhaps we need to consider this idea—if only briefly. Because sometimes we can become so bogged down in who we *think* we are; or who we've *always* been; or who we *suppose* we'll be tomorrow, that we completely lose sight of all the opportunities to change, grow, and actually become something far better and much more satisfying *today*. In the midst of our hectic schedules it's difficult to notice that seasons are rushing by us— and we're not necessarily evolving as fully as we could be.

But if we look around us to nature, we can see that God's creation is reinvented almost daily. Trees bud, then blossom, then turn leafy green, then bear fruit and move into lovely autumn colors. . . . So, why would we think our lives must always remain the same? Why shouldn't we, like a butterfly, be open to some beautiful forms of metamorphosis as well?

FOR FURTHER REFLECTION

Think about ways that you'd like to be different. Then consider, realistically, what it would take to incorporate some of these changes into your life—today, not in some distant season. Finally, bring these desires before God and ask for His guidance and blessing.

PRAYER

*Dear Lord, there are things about myself that I'd like to change.
But I don't always know where or how to start.
Please, help me to become everything You want me to be. Amen*

A Healthy Habitat

*Honor and majesty are before him; strength and beauty
are in his sanctuary.*

—Psalm 96:6

When we're choosing to convert our lives from those of stress, chaos, confusion . . . to ones of peace, calmness, serenity . . . we need to remember it's important to change our environment as well. For how can we help but feel overwhelmed if we dwell amongst a jumble of disorder and clutter? We need to transform where we live and work.

Small things like clearing and organizing our workspace; placing a small vase of fresh flowers nearby; lighting an aromatic candle; playing soft music . . . can do wonders to reduce our sense of being overwhelmed. In our homes, we can simplify and streamline (get rid of what we don't need!) and then make sure we add loving touches of beauty in the form of soothing colors, comforting textures, fragrant smells, pleasant sounds—all working to create a habitat that's like an invigorating health tonic for the soul.

FOR FURTHER REFLECTION

Take a sharp look at your environment. Does it promote a feeling of peace and well being, or does it make you feel anxious and overwhelmed? Begin by eliminating unnecessary clutter. Then bring in a touch of beauty—something that makes you smile and say "ahhh."

PRAYER

Loving Creator, help me to remember the beautiful and orderly world You've designed for us, and show me some small ways I can do the same for my environment. Amen

Peace Amidst Chaos

Be still, and know that I am God!

—Psalm 46:10

Although we *can* control some smaller things within our environment at work and home, we *cannot* control everything. And to fool ourselves into believing we can will only invite overwhelming frustration—and we don't need that! So, let's learn to accept that most elements of life are simply beyond our external control. However, that doesn't mean these challenges are beyond our *internal* control—because we don't have to let life's stress get to us.

We can maintain a peaceful spirit in the midst of chaos—be the calm center while the storm whirls all around. *But only with God.* For if we come before God and invite His peace into our hearts, He can sustain us through the most stressful and trying times. For *His* is the kind of peace that knows no limits. And He gives His peace to all who ask.

FOR FURTHER REFLECTION

Consider the stress-inducing things in your life that you cannot control. Admit to yourself and to God that they are beyond you. Then ask God to fill you with His peace—a peace unlike any other—whenever you feel overwhelmed.

PRAYER

Dear God, I admit there are all kinds of things in my life that I cannot control, but I'm tired of being caught up by them. Please, fill me with Your perfect peace. Amen

. . . The Ones You Love

I give you a new commandment, that you love one another.
Just as I have loved you, you also should love one another.
—John 13:34

We all know what a capacity we have to hurt those we love the most. And this seems to happen even more frequently when we're suffering from things like stress and overwhelming circumstances. It's probably because we feel more free to "let our hair down" around those we love (we know they love us and will forgive us eventually). But isn't it a shame that we must make them suffer like that?

But as we make strides in our campaign to overcome being overwhelmed, then our loved ones will surely benefit too. They'll begin to see a difference in how we react and relate to them. And perhaps they'll all exhale a big sigh of relief. But we may need to explain to them what we're trying to do, so they can support us in our efforts. And we may need to apologize for some of the hurts we've dealt them in the past, and invite them to team up with us as we continue to grow.

FOR FURTHER REFLECTION

Consider the people closest to you—those you love the most. In the past, has your stress level hurt them? Have you asked for their forgiveness? Have you told them about the ways you are trying to change now? Have you invited them to partner with you?

PRAYER

God of love, please forgive me for hurting the ones I love.
Help me to make amends with them. Please, bring our hearts
together in an exciting new way. Amen

A High Price to Pay

He must turn from evil and do good;
he must seek peace and pursue it.

—1 Peter 3:11

Perhaps as an inoculation (or form of health insurance) against ever returning to our old stressful ways, we need to be reminded of what a high price one might pay to continue in a lifestyle that's overwhelming. Of course, there are the obvious negative factors such as anxiety, unhappiness, worry, tension, confusion, distractions, and divisions.

But there are even worse effects to our physical well being— some of them long-term and life threatening: high blood pressure, heart disease, stroke, and numerous other maladies. There are even some physicians who believe *every* illness is stress-related in one way or another. Remembering this might keep us from slipping back into our old ways. For stress comes with a high price—who can afford it?

FOR FURTHER REFLECTION

Take a moment to remember why you've been making some choices to change the way you live and think. Thank God that you are making the progress you've made. And promise yourself and God that you'll continue along this healthier path of life.

PRAYER

Thank You, God, for all You do in my life! Thank You for saving me from all sorts of pain that I might have unwittingly inflicted upon myself. Help me to stay on track. Amen

Identity Crunched

"But what about you?" he asked. "Who do you say I am?"
—Mark 8:29

Those of us who have battled stress, anxiety, and being overwhelmed may tend to see ourselves in some particular ways. We may perceive ourselves as people who are always running fast, often late, trying too hard, usually tired, overworked, underappreciated . . . all sorts of things. But usually not positive things. In other words, our image may be skewed by who we *think* we are. But if we're trying to change all that, then we may need to make an adjustment as to how we see ourselves, as well as how others see us.

So, perhaps it's time to start building another identity. One that is more true to who we really are—who we're becoming. Maybe we need to envision such qualities as calmness, peacefulness, gladness, joyfulness. Perhaps we need to present ourselves with confidence, grace, competence, true humility, and self-control.

FOR FURTHER REFLECTION

Begin to think of who it is you're becoming. List the traits you already see in yourself and those you would like to see. As you move through your day, keep these qualities in mind, and practice showing others this new image until it becomes a habit.

PRAYER

Dear Lord, You are changing me. Hopefully I am becoming more like You. Help me to cooperate, and to perceive myself more clearly. Change my self-image. Amen

Disengaging

*Do not let the floodwaters engulf me or the depths swallow me up
or the pit close its mouth over me.*

—Psalm 69:15

Many of us who've dealt with being overwhelmed may need to admit that we have a tendency to care too much, to become overly involved, or to carry too big of a load. It may be that we need to learn how to healthfully *disengage* upon occasion. To disengage means that we slightly distance ourselves from certain kinds of people and situations—the kinds that tend to pull us into conflict or problems that are unrelated to our own lives.

It's not that we don't want to help others, but sometimes we set ourselves up to be *emotional-baggage carriers* for them, when they probably need to be carrying their own bags. We become heavy laden, stressed out, and discouraged. And that's when we need to disengage and step away. Because if we go under, we can't save anyone else.

FOR FURTHER REFLECTION

Consider those relationships or situations that tend to pull you in and then sap all your emotional energy. Make a conscious decision to step away. Of course, you can pray for these people and offer encouragement. But, for their sake and yours, resist involvement.

PRAYER

*Please, God, show me when a relationship is harmful.
Teach me how to disengage myself without abandoning someone.
Help me to bring these burdens to You. Amen*

Time for Pleasures

For everything there is a season,
and a time for every matter under heaven.

—Ecclesiastes 3:1

When we live busy and demanding lives, it's easy to put off certain pleasures. Or maybe we think "pleasures" are frivolous or unnecessary—who has time? Maybe we're "martyr" types, or possibly, we don't even realize we're missing out. But when was the last time you enjoyed a long, luxurious soak in a fragrant bubble bath? When was the last time you read a really good book—just for the fun of it?

When did you last take a stroll, not for exercise, but for pure enjoyment? When did you last eat something simply because it delighted your senses? When did you last pause to admire the sky, or a perfect sunset? When did you last feel the wind in your hair? The sun on your shoulders? Listen to a bird sing with abandon?

FOR FURTHER REFLECTION

Be aware of the daily pleasures around you. Plan something that feels like a real treat today. Perhaps it's a walk through the park; or an extended break with a special snack; or a cruise through the corner antique store; or a nice, long bubble bath at the end of the day.

PRAYER

Precious Lord, remind me that it's okay to relax and enjoy myself. Show me some simple ways I can refresh myself daily. Please, help restore my joy and my youth! Amen

Refining Your Calendar

Teach us to number our days aright,
that we may gain a heart of wisdom.

—Psalm 90:12

Do you have a tendency to pack as much as you possibly can into your calendar? Many of us overwhelmed types do. It's almost as if we think we'll be presented with some sort of achievement award for accomplishing more than anyone else (and more than is humanly possible) in one week. But what we'll really receive are things like headaches, worry lines, and heartburn.

So perhaps it's time (once again) to take a discerning look at our calendars. Is everything on there really necessary? Is it helpful? Is it good? Does it add stress? Should we eliminate it? What can be erased and never missed? Just because we "have time" to do something doesn't necessarily mean it needs to be done. And, perhaps most importantly, have we scheduled some things that are fun and enjoyable?

FOR FURTHER REFLECTION

Take a long, hard look at your calendar. Perhaps start by reviewing the previous month. Does it seem overly hectic and full? Ask yourself how much of this is truly necessary. How much of this is part of your old "performer" nature? Eliminate and simplify!

PRAYER

Dear God, teach me to number my days wisely.
Help me to schedule some "down times." Show me ways
to simplify my calendar and live more freely. Amen

Running on Empty?

*May the Lord direct your hearts to the love of God
and to the steadfastness of Christ.*

—2 Thessalonians 3:5

"Overachievers" tend to take delight in raising the expectation bar higher and higher. There are many theories for why we do this, but it usually boils down to a somewhat skewed sense of self-esteem. In other words, it just makes us feel good. Or at least we think we feel good, for the moment anyway. But in the long run, when we continue trying to keep up a frantic and unrealistic pace, we usually discover that our resources of energy are sadly depleted and we are, in fact, running on empty.

Perhaps we're running on empty because we're operating on our own energies instead of God's. And perhaps we're running on our own energies because we're running a race that God never chose for us. But if we run the race that God sets before us, He'll give us the stuff we need to finish—victoriously!

FOR FURTHER REFLECTION

Are you feeling drained in any way? Are you running on empty? And, if so, are you even running in the right direction? Redirect your focus onto God and the way He's leading you. Ask Him to fill you with His strength and get you going in the right way.

PRAYER

Lord Jesus, I confess, I sometimes feel depleted and tired and worn out. I need You to fill me with Your energy—Your strength, wisdom, grace, love, humility. Amen

The Tortoise and the Hare

Therefore, since we are surrounded by such a great cloud of witnesses, let us throw off everything that hinders and the sin that so easily entangles, and let us run with perseverance the race marked out for us.

—Hebrews 12:1

We've all heard that old fable of that famous turtle and rabbit that agreed to a footrace. But which of these animals do we relate to? Most likely, the rabbit, because we too try to run fast; and often we have false confidence in our speed and ability, and besides we like to win!

But what can we learn from the plodding tortoise? We can be reminded of the need to pace ourselves. Obviously, he didn't win the race by just sitting around. He put one foot in front of the other and just kept going. We can be reminded that the fastest one doesn't always win. Or that pride comes before the fall. But perhaps most importantly, we can learn the value of persistence—of never giving up!

FOR FURTHER REFLECTION

Consider the pace you've been maintaining in life lately. Is it too fast to keep up like this indefinitely? Is it stop and start—jumpy and bumpy? Is your focus only on breaking big records? Or are you simply trying to complete the race to the best of your ability?

PRAYER

Father in heaven, teach me how to pace myself in this race of life. Only You know how long it will be and where the finish line lies. Please, coach me along the way. Amen

Preventing a Breakdown

You restored me to health and let me live.

—Isaiah 38:16

We've already been reminded about the high cost our physical bodies can pay when we live with unchecked areas of stress in our lives. But we need to consider our mental health as well. The ultimate cost of being continually overwhelmed without any relief can be a very real and debilitating emotional breakdown. It's simply the mind's way of saying "Gimme a break!"

But, thankfully, we can prevent these types of breakdowns by giving ourselves lots of little breaks along the way. This means scheduling daily times when we can unwind and relax. How about taking a "mini" vacation (an unexpected day or weekend off) where we allow ourselves an extended escape from the demands of daily life? For taking a much-needed break now is a lot better than having a breakdown later.

FOR FURTHER REFLECTION

Ask yourself (yes, again!): Are you taking a sufficient amount of time for breaks? Daily? Do you allow for down time at the end of your day? Do you need a "mini" vacation? Or an even longer one? Promise that you'll give yourself the breaks you need.

PRAYER

Gentle Creator, show me when and how to give myself better breaks. Help me to realize that I am not invincible and that I must take care of my needs in order to help others. Amen

Don't Neglect Yourself

*The Lord is my rock, my fortress and my deliverer; my God is my
rock, in whom I take refuge. He is my shield and the horn
of my salvation, my stronghold.*

—Psalm 18:2

Sometimes we erroneously think we're being somewhat heroic to
put our needs behind everyone else's. It's not that our needs should
always come first, but on the other hand, they shouldn't always be
last either. Consider the instructions given regarding oxygen
masks before a jet takes off. The flight attendant patiently explains
that the masks will fall from the ceiling compartments, and if you
are traveling with someone who needs your help, make sure you
put on your oxygen mask *first*. Then and *only* then, do you attend
to the needs of the other person.

The reason is that without your own mask in place, you might
pass out before you get a chance to help the other person. And
then you'll both be in serious trouble. So, the point is, let's not
neglect ourselves. For if we do, all will suffer.

FOR FURTHER REFLECTION

*Consider where you've placed your own needs on your priority list.
Which, if any, needs have you been neglectful of in the past? What
are some specific ways you can change your thinking in this area?
Promise yourself that you will take care of your own needs.*

PRAYER

*Dear Lord, show me that it's not selfish to take better care of myself.
Help me to recognize my own needs, and to make a plan
to meet them. Amen*

Living Well

*Every good and perfect gift is from above, coming down from the
Father of the heavenly lights, who does not change like
shifting shadows.*

—James 1:17

A surefire way to become totally overwhelmed is to attempt to
model ourselves and our homes on one of the many homestyle
mavens gracing the television airwaves or the magazine racks.
Trying to live up to anyone else's image or expectations in any area
of life is bound to be frustrating if only because we're following the
beat of their drum instead of listening to the beat of our own
hearts—a song written there by God. Sure, all that glossy
perfection and beauty looks pretty good on TV or at the
newsstand, but to duplicate someone else's idea of fashionable may
suffocate all the unique style God has planted in you.

Still, it doesn't mean that we can't get plenty of wonderful ideas
and suggestions from the "experts." But we don't have to drive
ourselves nuts trying to attain some highly detailed level of décor,
fashion, or culinary mastery all by ourselves—remember, the folks
that put these enviable projects together may have dozens of
people working behind the scenes to make it all look perfect.

FOR FURTHER REFLECTION

*Allow yourself the luxury of letting unrealistic or perfectionist
expectations slip away. It doesn't mean you must sacrifice beauty or
pleasure, but that you will seek them in easier and simpler ways.
Choose to overlook small imperfections and focus on the good.*

PRAYER

*Help me, God, to remember that true perfection can be found only
in You. Show me ways I need to "let some things go." Help me to
enjoy simple beauty and pleasures. Amen*

A New Image

Do not lie to each other, since you have taken off your old self with its practices and have put on the new self, which is being renewed in knowledge in the image of its Creator.

—Colossians 3:9, 10

As we're attempting to impart some healthy change into our lives, we may notice that our own image is changing as well. Perhaps it's in a more peaceful countenance. Maybe someone's mentioned how we seem more relaxed and at ease these days. It seems inevitable that our outward appearance will be altered by our inward transformation.

And it's important that we welcome these changes, that we cooperate with this new image that's slowly emerging. To do so, we need to begin seeing ourselves differently too. Let's take a deep breath and remember that we have more control in our life. Let's walk with fresh confidence. Let's stand straight, shoulders back, now free from old weights we once carried. Sure, these are just small physical things, but they can send big messages. For as we perceive ourselves differently, so will those around us.

FOR FURTHER REFLECTION

Consider the ways you've been changing lately. Look in the mirror and remind yourself of how much you've transformed. Stand taller and straighter. Breathe deeply. Smile more. And see if others don't start noticing something different about you too!

PRAYER

King of heaven, help me to show on the outside the successes I'm experiencing on the inside. Help me to see myself as You do, and to live like I'm really a child of the King! Amen

A Servant's Heart

But as for me and my household, we will serve the Lord.

—Joshua 24:15

Can you remember a time when you felt down and out and someone—someone who seemed to have it fairly well together—reached out and helped you without making you feel inferior? Moments like that can crystallize in our hearts and minds, staying with us forever. But what are the chances we will ever be remembered in that way by someone else? Perhaps now, as we begin to feel less overwhelmed by life and, as a result, more confident, perhaps now we are ready to reach out to others with that kind of selfless love.

For the best way we can love others is to have the heart of a loyal servant—someone who's not seeking attention for himself, but simply wants to help another. It can happen in small or big ways. But when it happens we are transformed!

FOR FURTHER REFLECTION

Look for an opportunity to help someone today. This doesn't mean making a big commitment to a cause. Perhaps it's just letting a car merge into traffic before you. Or smiling at a cantankerous coworker. But don't do it so someone will notice you; just do it because you care. Then do it again!

PRAYER

Almighty God, please, help me to develop a servant's heart. Make me into the sort of person who helps others with kindness and true humility. Show me ways to do this. Amen

When It's Time to Stop

But they refused to listen, and turned a stubborn shoulder,
and stopped their ears in order not to hear.
—Zechariah 7:11

Sometimes it seems that those of us who've been stressed and overwhelmed have some old "stubborn" roots buried deep inside of us. Perhaps we even view this stubbornness as a good thing because we know how to "stick to it." And persistence is an admirable quality—at least up to a point. But there is another kind of stubborn persistence that borders along the lines of foolishness. That's when we don't know when to stop.

We get going on some project and suddenly all that matters is getting it done! We become obsessed with finishing, and often at the expense of those around us (sometimes the ones we love the most!). But if we can teach ourselves to let go; step back; take a deep breath; and know when to quit—everyone will be much better off. And then, perhaps later on, we can go back and attack the problem from a fresh angle. Or not!

FOR FURTHER REFLECTION

Consider some things that you've not been able to let go of. Is it possible that what you've thought of as persistence is really just stubborn pride? Practice the art of knowing when it's time to just stop. Then practice the self-control of doing it.

PRAYER

Kind Father in heaven, help me to know when it's time to stop.
Show me how my stubbornness is one way I don't trust You
enough. Then, help me to trust You more. Amen

Laughing Out Loud

He will yet fill your mouth with laughter,
and your lips with shouts of joy.

—Job 8:21

One of the all-time best stress relievers is a good, long, belly laugh. In fact, it's not uncommon for someone who's been overwhelmed with worry, grief, or anxiety to suddenly (and for almost no rational reason) burst out into what almost becomes a hysterical form of laughter. Perhaps it's just the body's way of saying, "Enough is enough! It's time to break loose!"

But maybe we can take the upper hand here and invite some good humor into our lives before we reach that near-breaking point. Life shouldn't be so serious that we neglect to welcome laughter and merriment. So, let's commit ourselves to make time to share a funny joke or story. Then let's laugh out loud, good and hard!

FOR FURTHER REFLECTION

Decide today to quit taking life so seriously, and take a walk on the lighter side. Be on the watch for any humor you might discover in your day. Keep an eye out for a funny joke. Smile more, be wittier, and enjoy a good laugh.

PRAYER

God of love, help me to develop a better sense of humor. And remind me that it's not only okay to laugh, but it's a good, healthy thing. Amen

Random Acts of Kindness

The Lord is good to all, and his compassion is over all that he has made.

—Psalm 145:9

As we move further away from those old sources of stress and anxiety, stepping back from what used to overwhelm us, we will become more and more equipped to share our renewed sense of joy and peace with others. And that's when we might discover the blessing of "random acts of kindness." Although we may also discover that these acts are really not so very random, but the results of pre-planned and strategic caring and sharing.

A "random act of kindness" is a good deed we do for someone else (although there's no law that says we can't treat *ourselves* to some kindness as well). The idea is that we do as many as possible, and hopefully the trend will catch on and create an epidemic. Some people pay the highway toll for the unknown car waiting behind them. Others anonymously donate scholarship money to a struggling student. These acts of kindness come in all shapes and sizes, but most find the best blessing is in the giving!

FOR FURTHER REFLECTION

Be on the watch for any opportunity that might come your way today to perform a "random act of kindness." The best "acts" are where you get no glory, someone else is happily surprised, and you get the reward of knowing you really helped someone, without wearing yourself out in the process.

PRAYER

Dear Lord, help me to look around me today and to notice someone in need. Then show me how I can best meet that need in a kind and loving way. Amen

God's Perfect Timing

For every matter has its time and way, although the troubles of mortals lie heavy upon them.
—Ecclesiastes 8:6

Sometimes we want something to happen—and like a child eager to unwrap a birthday present—we want it to happen *now!* And often this kind of impatient thinking can be quite overwhelming. We become frustrated by having to wait for something that we think should've been here minutes, hours, days, or even years ago. But that's only because we're operating on our own sense of timing. Not God's.

But God's timing is perfect. Just look at the way nature works its way through the seasons and you'll see it. Or consider the way a baby grows and rests in the womb until just the right time to emerge into this world. But unfortunately, we seldom see things from God's eternal perspective. And we get tired of waiting. But this is where trust comes in—we can rely on trust and faith to believe that God's timing for our lives is perfect.

FOR FURTHER REFLECTION

Acknowledge that it's easy to become impatient. But be aware of how your impatience only adds frustration to what is probably an uncontrollable circumstance. Try to consider the timing God has in mind the next time you must wait. Focus your thoughts on something positive and calming as you wait.

PRAYER

Dear God, I admit that I can be pretty impatient.
Help me to understand that You may have reasons for making me wait.
Maybe You just want me to slow down and notice
the world around me. Amen

Streamline Your Day

The thief comes only to steal and kill and destroy.
I came that they may have life, and have it abundantly.
—John 10:10

We can always find ways to simplify and streamline our lives. Whether we want to save time or energy, or preserve our inner peace—if we could just streamline a bit by eliminating the *unnecessary* we'd be better off. This might mean deciding if an errand is really necessary before we run it; or foregoing certain activities that we weren't really thrilled about having to participate in anyway. It could even be a matter of just throwing away some of the clutter that's been building up in the living room. As we remove unessential elements from our lives, they get a little simpler.

Consider some of your daily routines and ask yourself whether all you do, each step you take, is *really* necessary. Would your day be any less fulfilling if you deleted a thing or two? Are there errands that can be combined, or activities you could do once a week instead of once a day? Consider all your options, and see where you can cut back and streamline. Then do it!

FOR FURTHER REFLECTION

Carefully examine how you spend your time. Are some of your daily tasks unnecessary, redundant, wasteful? Think of new ways to do old things. If you know someone who practices good time management—ask him or her for some helpful tips.

PRAYER

Sometimes, God, I don't even notice the ways I'm wasting precious time. Please show me how I can streamline my life so that I might enjoy more quality time. Amen

A Breath of Prayer

Rejoice always, pray without ceasing, give thanks in all circumstances; for this is the will of God in Christ Jesus for you.
—1 Thessalonians 5:16-18

No one likes to admit it, but sometimes it's easy to forget to pray. Perhaps we think we can pray only in the quiet of the morning, or before a meal, or when we go to bed at night. And yet, distractions come (even at these times) and before we know it a big chunk of time has passed and we realize we haven't prayed for ages.

But God is *always* listening. He's available every minute of the day and night—and He's eager to connect with us. So, perhaps it's time we learned to simply "breathe" a prayer. As we're moving through traffic, or riding in a crowded elevator; as we're taking the kids to soccer practice, or waiting at the dentist's office, we can, as easily as breathing, utter a silent prayer of thanks and adoration, or even a plea for help. And we can do it again and again, throughout the day.

FOR FURTHER REFLECTION

Think about your prayer life and consider if there's room for improvement. Then practice the art of breathing a prayer. For instance, with each slow breath form the words, "I love You, Lord," in your mind. Or, "Thank You, Most High."

PRAYER

Dear Lord, please forgive me for not coming to You more regularly. Teach me that prayer can be as simple as breathing and that to pray without ceasing can make for vast improvements in my day and my life. Remind me that You're always listening. Amen

100 Years from Now

In this way they will lay up treasure for themselves as a firm foundation for the coming age, so that they may take hold of the life that is truly life.

—1 Timothy 6:19

Have you ever felt overwhelmed by what feels like a totally perplexing question, and you're just not sure how to answer, or which way to go? Sometimes part of the problem is that *every* choice seems like a good one, and we become hung up on which is the *best* choice. When that happens, perhaps we should consider the impact this choice will have in the future. If what we're deciding won't matter one iota 100 years from now, or for that matter, even two weeks from now, we might decide it's not worth fretting about quite so much. Suddenly, many of the most nagging problems are diminished. Of course, there will always be important decisions to be made that will have long-term consequences, but think of the resources we've freed up to give them the attention they deserve!

While not all decisions can be weighed using the 100-year rule, it does help us put into perspective many of trivial issues (like which wallpaper pattern to pick, or which eyeglasses look best, or which dish to prepare for the Christmas party) we allow to clutter up our minds. And it reminds us of what our priorities should be, and which issues are the ones that should really concern us.

FOR FURTHER REFLECTION

Keep this 100-year thought in mind today as you face some of your regular daily problems. See if it makes you think differently or handle things in a more thoughtful and caring way.

PRAYER

Gracious Father, help me to know what's really important and what's not. I tend to get so caught up in the minutia. Show me the issues that really matter to You. Amen

Your Secret Dream

He said to them, "Listen to this dream that I dreamed."
—Genesis 37:6

Perhaps you don't think you have a secret dream. Or perhaps you've simply forgotten it. Or maybe it seems so childish and impossible that you've given up on ever achieving it. But maybe it's time to remember that dream, and to ask yourself if there's something important you've left behind. For sometimes God gives us dreams and desires, and He's just waiting for us to call out to Him for the help to fulfill them.

Sometimes the dreams begin in childhood, sometimes later, and often they can seem fanciful or idealistic, not to mention impractical. But perhaps that's because they never mature from the infantile stage. Perhaps it's because we've buried them too deep. But maybe we need to allow ourselves the freedom to pull out these old dreams, shake off the dust, and give them a good long look. For some of us, they might even provide insight into just why we keep ourselves so incredibly busy all the time.

FOR FURTHER REFLECTION

Perhaps you're living your dream, but if not, try to remember what your greatest dreams and hopes were. What did you used to think you wanted to do? Prayerfully, consider this dream. Did you decide it was too farfetched and impossible? Is it reflected in your life today? Is there a chance that you've kept yourself overly busy in order to keep from pursuing your deepest desires?

PRAYER

Almighty God, help me to remember the dreams that You have given me. Then help me to bring these back to You and trust You to bring them to pass. Amen

Fail to Plan, Plan to Fail

Commit your work to the Lord,
and your plans will be established.

—Proverbs 16:3

We've probably all heard the old adage, "Failing to plan is like planning to fail." But, admittedly, our plans aren't always the smartest or the best. Yet to avoid making any plans at all is to be like a ship on a rough sea with no rudder to guide it.

But for those of us who are overwhelmed by our hectic schedules, it's easy to allow circumstances and demands to direct us through our day, rather than a well-conceived plan and attentiveness to God's guidance. And, of course, that brings on all sorts of frustrations and stress. We become like the ship being tossed back and forth by the waves. But a plan is like a map and compass to guide us—without it we are lost. And, of course, the best plans are those covered with lots of prayer!

FOR FURTHER REFLECTION

Take a little time to plan your day. You may want to write it out, not minute by minute, of course, but enough to make plain what you'd like to and what you need to accomplish. And don't forget to pray for God's guidance. Then see if your day goes better.

PRAYER

Dear God, I realize how wonderfully You have planned this world, and understand that there is room for better planning in my life. Please, help me to make good plans. Amen

Prioritize Your Life

For though I am absent from you in body, I am present with you in spirit and delight to see how orderly you are and how firm your faith in Christ is.

—Colossians 2:5

The things that seem the most pressing and urgent at the moment are very often not the most truly important things in life. Quite frequently, it's the trivial stuff that demands an unfair portion of our attention, energy, and time. Things like a stubborn fax machine, a careless coworker, or a long line at the checkout can eat up our days bit by bit. And sometimes those little irritations distract us from what *really* matters. That's when we need to stop and remember life's priorities (hopefully we're starting to think of them more regularly now).

While priorities differ for everyone, we're wise to keep God first. Then, hopefully, we'll list our closest loved ones next. But, since we're learning to not place our needs last, let's remember to put ourselves on our priority list as well. And finally, we'll list things like career, outreach, hobbies, and whatnot. We don't have to actually write them out, but sometimes it helps to see them in bold print.

FOR FURTHER REFLECTION

Remember what your priorities in life really are. Go ahead and list them out (if it helps). Then consider what's most important and the way you spend your time. Do you give more time and energy to the less important things? Are there changes you should make?

PRAYER

King of heaven, help me to know what's truly important in my life. Help me to keep You first, and to allow You to show me the order of everything else. Amen

Just Look Around

*We were under great pressure, far beyond our ability to endure,
so that we despaired even of life. Indeed, in our hearts we felt
the sentence of death. But this happened that we might not
rely on ourselves but on God, who raises the dead.*

—2 Corinthians 1:8, 9

Do you ever feel so pressured that you think you might actually explode? *Why is that?* Perhaps if we could all just pause for a moment and simply take a good long look around, we might figure out a few things. First of all, where do these pressures come from? From others or from ourselves? If they come from others, are they legitimate and worthy of our attention? Or is it just outside interference that needs to be ignored? If we're pressuring ourselves, is it for good reason? Or are we simply falling victim to old habits and a flawed way of thinking?

So, let's calmly look around and take inventory. With a calming deep breath, we can begin to see what's really going on. And as we use our best judgment, we can focus on what's really necessary, and allow the rest to wait its turn or just go away. And all along, we need to trust that God will deliver us from this crushing pressure.

FOR FURTHER REFLECTION

Decide to hone your powers of observation. Be watchful and aware of what's going on around you. Stay a step ahead of stress and pressure, by carefully sifting and sorting what needs your attention and what doesn't. Pray for wisdom and discernment.

PRAYER

*Precious Lord, help me to not only see what's around me,
but to see it with wisdom and discernment. Please, develop
an awareness in me to keep me on track. Amen*

Simplify, Simplify, Simplify

All who cleanse themselves of the things I have mentioned will become special utensils, dedicated and useful to the owner of the house, ready for every good work.

—2 Timothy 2:21

It seems to be our nature (as soon as we start feeling that life is under control) to take on more complications. And if we give in to this, we will quickly become overwhelmed all over again. The answer is to make simplification our motto. Simplify, simplify, simplify!

If we really want a fresh challenge—why not focus our newfound energies on plain old simplification? We can simplify by organizing our closet (getting rid of all excess), or eliminating clutter in our kitchen drawers (if we don't use it, lose it!). We can simplify by saying "no," canceling catalog subscriptions, putting ourselves on a "do not call" list, organizing storage spaces, finding a place for everything, and getting rid of everything that bogs us down. Because the truth is, it takes commitment and work to simplify our lives. But, oh, what a payoff! The peace, the calm, the simple beauty of order . . . it's worth working hard for.

FOR FURTHER REFLECTION

Decide to make simplification your motto. Of course, you won't become completely streamlined overnight, but whenever you're tempted to complicate your life with a new commitment, consider focusing that energy on simplifying in some very specific way. Start simple: clean out a drawer!

PRAYER

Merciful God, teach me how to simplify. Remind me that adding something new to my life doesn't always equal more. Help me to identify and remove all of my unnecessary clutter. Amen

A Quiet Heart

Do not adorn yourselves outwardly by braiding your hair,
and by wearing gold ornaments or fine clothing; rather,
let your adornment be the inner self with the lasting beauty of a
gentle and quiet spirit, which is very precious in God's sight.
—1 Peter 3:3, 4

One way we can nurture a calm spirit and a quiet heart within us is to allow ourselves a period of uninterrupted time—starting with as little as five minutes will do—each and every day for prayer, meditation, or reflection. The next step is to practice listening more and speaking less. It's amazing what we can learn by keeping our mouths closed. And it's said that even a fool will appear wise when he remains silent.

Although there's an art to having a quiet spirit, it's a learnable art. As we choose to embrace new habits like focusing our minds and spirits on hearing God, or listening to those around us, we are changed—transformed even.

FOR FURTHER REFLECTION

Do you long for a peaceful, inner calm—a quiet heart? Dedicate a few minutes each day to prayer or meditation. Then set up a reminder for yourself (a note on your computer, a string around your finger) that helps you to say less and to listen more.

PRAYER

Dear God, I want to develop that kind of quiet heart that can attune itself to You and those around me. Please, show me how to hear you more clearly. Amen

Dealing with Distraction

*But the Lord answered her, "Martha, Martha, you are worried
and distracted by many things; there is need of only one thing.
Mary has chosen the better part, which will not be
taken away from her."*

—Luke 10:41, 42

Distractions seem to be the order of the day. And, in reality, they
are a normal part of daily living. Telephones interrupt. Things get
misplaced. People need help. There's no escaping many of life's
distractions. But perhaps we can learn to differentiate between
kinds of distractions—to discern between those that must be
attended to, and those that are nothing more than annoyances.
And that might take prayer and practice.

But we can avoid some distractions by keeping our priorities
(whether at work or at home) in mind. And when certain
interruptions or distractions hit, we can weigh them against these
priorities, then decide how to deal with them accordingly. And, of
course, we can always invite God's help to know the difference.

FOR FURTHER REFLECTION

*Focus on your priorities today. Then be aware when distractions
come, asking yourself if you must give them your attention or not.
Pray for discernment to know the difference between those that
warrant your attention and those that do not.*

PRAYER

*Eternal God, help me to be wise when it comes to things that
distract me. Please, give me Your discernment to deal with
whatever comes my way today. Amen*

Let Your Light Shine

*No one after lighting a lamp puts it under the bushel basket,
but on the lampstand, and it gives light to all in the house.*
—Matthew 5:15

As we strive for a calmer, more peaceful sort of life, it might be easy to become somewhat self-focused at first. For a time, we may have to be more concerned with our own needs in order to eventually become more effective in dealing with the needs of others. But as we become stronger and more in control of our lives, we can begin to see that taking care of ourselves is truly one of the most self-*less* things we can do for others.

When we are fit and happy and living well-balanced lives we are a joy for everyone to behold. No more moaning about our horrible workload, no more falling asleep in the middle of sentences, no more stress-related illnesses—instead the time spent with friends and family is full of laughter and smiles and energy. When we're with them we're able to give our full attention to our loved ones, and as a result we are able to receive all the love we haven't always been available for in the past, when we were stressed to the max.

FOR FURTHER REFLECTION

Think about ways you can show your beautiful, renewed spirit to the world. Look for opportunities to share a gracious word or a smile or a chance to lend a helping hand.

PRAYER

*Dear Lord, You have graciously given me so much.
Thank you for the countless reasons you give me every day to smile and laugh with those around me and to have a joyful heart. Amen*

Why Put It Off?

God has said, "Never will I leave you; never will I forsake you."
So we say with confidence, "The Lord is my helper; I will not
be afraid. What can man do to me?"
—Hebrews 13:5, 6

Why do we procrastinate? Perhaps it's because we already have too much on our plates, or we think it will be easier to handle it later. Sometimes we put things off because we're worried that we'll be unable to finish, so why even start? When it's a project we think we'll enjoy, our delay may actually be related to our need for a break. We may want to wait until we can savor the job, as if it's a reward from our usual drudgery—but of course, the "perfect" time to do it never comes. But most often, the battle we wage may well be only in our minds. Have you ever noticed how when you delay something inevitable it seems to grow more ominous and unattainable with each passing day? Fear can be paralyzing.

But if we can just force ourselves to begin, and take the assignment one step at a time, it *will* get done eventually. And when it does we'll know we've accomplished a difficult task, and if we've done that we can do the other things before us, too.

FOR FURTHER REFLECTION

Is there something you're putting off that needs to be done? Is it because it feels too overwhelming to tackle? Remind yourself that you may not be seeing it correctly, and then decide that you will begin on it without further procrastination.

PRAYER

Gracious Lord, help me to not put off until tomorrow what I know I can, and must, start today. Give me the wisdom and strength to stay on task and not procrastinate, knowing that You will help me in all I do. Amen

It's Okay to Do Nothing

Six days you shall work, but on the seventh day you shall rest;
even in plowing time and harvest time you shall rest.

—Exodus 34:21

Sometimes we can be so hard on ourselves. Maybe it's our perfectionist nature, or our tendency to overachieve. But how often do we allow ourselves to simply rest and relax and do absolutely *nothing*? Maybe we had a grandmother who said it was wrong "to sit around and do nothing," or maybe it just seems like a senseless waste of time to those of us who are used to running— and running fast.

But, oh, how we need those down times of total (and guilt-free!) freedom to just sit in a rocking chair and simply rock. Or to flop down on our backs and just stare at the sky. Or to empty our minds and enjoy the silence. It's really okay to do nothing sometimes. In fact, there are times when doing nothing is the best thing you can do. And, the truth is, most of us don't do it nearly enough.

FOR FURTHER REFLECTION

Allow yourself a moment today to do absolutely nothing. Recognize that it might be hard. You may struggle with guilt, or the sudden urge to fill the void of nothingness with something of "more value." But control yourself and enjoy a moment of no pressure.

PRAYER

Dear God, after creating the world, You took a day to rest.
Help me to know when and how to relax and do nothing simply
for the purpose of refreshing my soul. Amen

Fighting Fear

God is our refuge and strength, an ever-present help in trouble.
Therefore we will not fear, though the earth give way and the
mountains fall into the heart of the sea, though its waters roar
and foam and the mountains quake with their surging.

—Psalm 46:1-3

We sometimes fail to realize how easily we can overwhelm ourselves with absolutely no help from the outside. Usually it begins with worry (often unfounded) and slowly that can grow into anxiety (sometimes without our realization) and left unchecked it can turn into a form of real, live fear. Maybe it's the fear we can't handle something, or that we might not do something well enough, or that we might actually fail. But that fear, left to itself, can be pretty debilitating. And left untended, it can even transform itself into panic attacks—the kind that wake us up in the middle of the night.

But we can also learn to recognize fear's roots, and deal with them swiftly, before they take hold. In other words, "the only thing we have to fear is fear itself." As we trust God, instead of worrying, our anxiety levels drop, and our unwarranted fears flee.

FOR FURTHER REFLECTION

Do certain situations or challenges cause you to worry or become anxious? Remind yourself that if you feel this way, it's time to ask God, and then trust Him, to help you. Recognize how unfounded fear is a roadblock to your destination. Just knock it down!

PRAYER

Almighty God, help me to give my worries and anxieties to You, and to trust that You are taking care of me. Please, keep my heart free from debilitating fears. Amen

Strength for the Day

Even youths grow tired and weary, and young men stumble and
fall; but those who hope in the Lord will renew their strength.
They will soar on wings like eagles; they will run and not grow
weary, they will walk and not be faint.
—Isaiah 40:30, 31

You know that kind of day—the dog chews up one of your new boots, the traffic is snarled all along the interstate, and then you can't even get online to access an important document that you need right away—and suddenly you find yourself wondering how many more days like this you can survive. Perhaps that's when we need to remember to take life *one day at a time*. Because, the fact is, it's just too difficult to consider all we'll require to get us through this thing called life, and still emerge in one piece.

We just need to remember that God has all that we need, not only to survive this torturous day, but to come through it with flying colors! He knows we are weak (He made us that way to remind us we need Him). He's waiting for us to ask so He can give us the strength we need for the day.

FOR FURTHER REFLECTION

Realize and admit that you, by nature, have a lot of weak areas in your life. Then come before God and ask Him to strengthen you, supernaturally. Ask Him to give you the strength you need to live this day to the fullest and best of your ability!

PRAYER

Lord Jesus, I confess that I'm weak. And sometimes I am easily overwhelmed. Please, give me Your strength—enough to get me through this day—and to glorify You! Amen

Friend or Foe?

This God—his way is perfect; the promise of the Lord proves true;
he is a shield for all who take refuge in him.

—2 Samuel 22:31

An ironically complicated area of life, and one that can bring on real frustration, is that of friendship. Sometimes it's tough to know exactly who our friends are. You may have been friends with Susan for years, but after every phone conversation with her, you hang up feeling guilty, or unhappy, or just plain stressed. Is this a healthy relationship? That's why we need to discern with whom we trust our hearts. We need to learn to recognize the friends who are true and loyal, and the ones we may need to guard ourselves against.

Not that some "friends" are enemies, exactly, but we should understand what we can and cannot expect from certain relationships. As a result, we don't love these "stress-inducing" friends any less, but we learn to control how much power they exert in our lives. We don't allow them to throw us off balance or overwhelm us.

FOR FURTHER REFLECTION

Consider who your friends are. Which ones are the most loyal and trustworthy? Which ones have brought more pain and frustration into your life? How can you be a good friend, and yet protect yourself in some ways? Show appreciation to a good, loyal friend.

PRAYER

Loving Father, help me to be wise when it comes to friends.
Show me the ones I can trust with deeper areas of my heart,
and those with whom I should be more careful. Amen

Waiting Patiently

I waited patiently for the Lord;
he turned to me and heard my cry.

—Psalm 40:1

Have you noticed that patience isn't a highly esteemed attribute in our current culture? Not in this age of fast food, speedy service, instant mixes, quicker connections. . . . It sometimes seems as if patience has become a nearly extinct virtue. To have to wait for something is almost an insult these days. We tap our toes as we wait in line. We repeatedly punch the buttons as we wait for the elevator. We hang up when we get placed on hold. We have all but forgotten the art of waiting patiently. But what we don't realize is that our impatience costs us something. It raises blood pressure, makes us feel uptight, wastes our emotions, and depletes us of good energy. But when we practice patience, we reap all sorts of benefits, not the least of which are self-control, peace, and inner joy, and the sure knowledge that God will answer our cry.

FOR FURTHER REFLECTION

Do you struggle with patience sometimes? List some specific areas where you feel challenged in this area. Now consider how you feel during these times of impatience. Do you enjoy these feelings? Decide today that you will practice patience.

PRAYER

God, I know I need to be more patient, but sometimes I don't even know how. Please, show me. Help me to come directly to You when I need patience. Amen

Divine "Interruptions"

See, I have refined you, though not as silver;
I have tested you in the furnace of affliction.

—Isaiah 48:10

Sometimes we're whizzing through our day, and everything seems to be tracking well, things are getting done, and we're really feeling a sense of control and accomplishment. Then WHAM— something totally throws us off course. And usually it's something we cannot avoid, something far beyond our control. Maybe it's a sick child, or a flat tire, or downed computer. But whatever it is, it stops us cold.

Perhaps we should consider this a "divine interruption." Perhaps we should look up to God and say, "Okay, now what?" Because, undoubtedly, there's a lesson to be learned, someone to be helped, a situation to resolve. And these are often those defining moments that can really make life a beautiful thing! So let's learn to embrace these divine interruptions, knowing that we will be stronger when we're done.

FOR FURTHER REFLECTION

Consider what is and is not within your control. Realize that when something happens (beyond your control) something that totally throws you off course—there is probably something significant to be learned there. Consider it a "divine interruption."

PRAYER

Remind me, Lord, that I can exhibit self-control in all areas of my life, even when external circumstances are beyond my control.
Help me to see these times as opportunities for me to stretch and learn, and remind me to call upon You for help when this happens.
Amen

A Centered Life

For the Lamb at the center of the throne will be
their shepherd; he will lead them to springs
of living water. And God will wipe away
every tear from their eyes.

—Revelation 7:17

Don't we all long to be that person who (seemingly) has it all together? The one who cruises through life with a peaceful countenance. The one who has the right words to say, who smiles in the face of trouble, whose socks match. If this person existed (because we have imagined him), we might describe him as very "centered."

But can we be centered too? And what does it really mean? Perhaps it means we need God to be in the center of our lives. That we need to be seeking Him daily. Inviting Him to show us how to live, and asking Him to give us the stuff to do it with. Then we would be centered. *Centered on God.*

FOR FURTHER REFLECTION

What's in the center of your life right now? Your job? Your family? Yourself? Or are you centered on God? Acknowledge that when you place God in the center, everything else will fall into its right place and life will begin to make sense. Center yourself on God.

PRAYER

God of love, show me how to keep You as the central and most important force within my life. I trust You to lead and direct me. Let me be centered on You. Amen

Destressing (12 Steps)

The Lord will guide you always.

1. We admit we cannot control all circumstances in our lives.
2. We believe that God controls the universe and wants to interact with us.
3. We make a decision to surrender our lives and our wills to God.
4. We take a long, honest, investigative look at our personal lives.
5. We admit to perfectionism, trying too hard, misplaced priorities, wrong values.
6. We make a commitment to change and simplify our lives.
7. We make a commitment to take better care of ourselves.
8. We make a commitment to slow down, enjoy life, laugh more, worry less.
9. We seek through prayer and meditation to increase our contact with God.
10. We seek to reach out and interact more lovingly to those dear to us.
11. We commit to forgive ourselves and others who've hurt us.
12. We commit to share what we've learned with others who are overwhelmed.

FOR FURTHER REFLECTION

Consider the twelve steps to destressing above. Do they resound with you? Copy these steps onto paper (editing as necessary to make them ring true for you) and post them where you can reread them on a regular basis. Use the twelve steps as a guideline (not the law) for moving away from stress and anxiety.

PRAYER

Help me, God, to move, one step at a time, toward the peace you want me to have. Guide each of my steps. Amen

Small Sacrifices, Big Rewards

*Through Jesus, therefore, let us continually offer to God
a sacrifice of praise—the fruit of lips that confess his name.*
—Hebrews 13:15

As we focus on becoming stress-free, we'll discover a few helpful hints along the way. Of course, not everything works for everyone. But we'll often find that giving up certain things will alleviate stress. For instance, we might want to consider giving up caffeine, or tobacco, or refined sugar. Or we might want to give up some time to exercise more.

We may need to examine in depth personal habits like diet and sleep. The key to eliminating stress is *balance*. A balanced and healthy diet, and a balance of sleep and activity. Because being out of balance heaps on additional stress. But the reward of making these personal changes is that we'll feel better. We'll have more energy, more ability to cope with the daily stresses that are beyond our control.

FOR FURTHER REFLECTION

Honestly consider your personal habits. Are there things you don't want to "give up" that are adding additional and unnecessary stress to your life? Are you willing to bring these things before God (start with one thing) and ask what He thinks?

PRAYER

*Dear Lord, please show me if there's something in my life,
some habit that I'm attached to, that's bringing me extra stress.
Strengthen me to deal with it. Amen*

The "Good Life"

No, we speak of God's secret wisdom, a wisdom that has been hidden and that God destined for our glory before time began.
—1 Corinthians 2:7

Don't we all long for the "good life"? But what is it really? For some of us the good life might be selling everything we own and moving to Kenya to be missionaries. For others it might be spending time with our grandchildren and watching them grow. It's totally different for each of us—it's as unique as we are. But when we become consumed by the whirlwinds of activity in our lives, we may lose sight of the good life that God has meant for us.

But, thankfully, we can wake up every morning knowing that God wants to guide us anew to the life we're meant to live. He alone has the right key for us—and we can ask Him to use it to open that door to our destiny!

FOR FURTHER REFLECTION

Somewhere inside of you is a longing for the "good life." Perhaps it's wrapped in many layers and you're not even sure which one is right. Spend some time thinking and praying and listening to your heart about what you believe your "good life" might be.

PRAYER

Merciful God, I believe You want me to live the "good life." And maybe I'm already partially there. But I invite You to show me more, help me to understand, and take me where you want me to be. Thank you for your never-failing compassions.
Amen

Finding the Funny

Sarah said, "God has brought me laughter, and everyone
who hears about this will laugh with me."
—Genesis 21:6

People who are overly stressed may tend to miss the humor in
everyday situations. And yet it is there—often just a smile or a
giggle away. As long as we're not too uptight to get it. Sometimes
we need to simply laugh at ourselves and the way we tend to take
life much too seriously. Sometimes we need to just sit back and
watch a funny movie.

But however we do it, we need to begin recognizing what's good
and humorous and lighthearted within our very own lives. Because
it's always there—if we're looking. And if we're having a really
tough time, it can help to be with a jovial friend—one who knows
how to really laugh and is gifted at merriment. Because nothing can
relieve the stress more quickly and easily than a good laugh.

FOR FURTHER REFLECTION

Decide to quit taking life so seriously. Be on the lookout for anything
that strikes you as amusing. Maybe it's a quirky billboard, a
character on the street, something your pet did, or a funny memory.
Practice smiling more, then loosen up your lips and just laugh.

PRAYER

Dear God, You created hippos and monkeys, so I know You have a
good sense of humor. Please, help me to develop mine.
Fill me with Your joy and happiness. Amen

Don't Fret

Cast all your anxiety on him because he cares for you.
—1 Peter 5:7

Yes, there are very frightening things going on in the world, and there are big problems in our lives that can seem daunting, but what do we accomplish by worrying about them? And just think of the joy we lose worrying about even the *little* things. Why do we fuss and fret over trivialities, allowing them to unhinge us? If we choose to, we can just as easily let them go, almost unnoticed.

Over time we have developed the habit of overreacting to life's little problems. And before we realized what was happening, that habit became ingrained in us, and now seems as much a part of us as our names. And yet, we can learn to think differently. We can change our ways. But only with real determination and God's help.

FOR FURTHER REFLECTION

Try to pinpoint a certain pet peeve that always seems to make you come unglued. Then realize how senseless it is to waste your emotional energy on something so trivial. Then determine not to be undermined by it again.

PRAYER

Help me, God, to recognize those silly little things that push my buttons. Then give me the strength and self-control to remain cool and calm and to not overreact. Amen

Revised Mission Statement

And we know that in all things God works for the good of those who love him, who have been called according to his purpose.
—Romans 8:28

Well, it's been awhile since we first composed our mission statement. Remember that's where we actually wrote down what our life goals are and how we hope to achieve them. And hopefully, we've made some strides and changes and progress since then. But perhaps we've also made some new discoveries, and have thought of some new things that we'd like to add. Or perhaps there are some old things that no longer seem terribly vital or important. So, let's drag out that old mission statement and see if it needs some revisions.

For any good mission statement should be open to improvements. And keep in mind, it's usually more motivating when we form our goals into positive statements, sentences like: "I will strive to know God better," or "I will spend more time with my family."

FOR FURTHER REFLECTION

Reread that old mission statement (without being self-critical). Then underline the parts you agree with the most. Is there anything you want to cross out? Then rewrite the statement, and post it (once again) in a place where you're sure to see it regularly.

PRAYER

Dear Lord, I ask Your direction and blessing on this mission statement. Thank You for constantly molding me. Amen

A Cultural Thing

What does the worker gain from his toil?
—Ecclesiastes 3:9

Americans, perhaps more than people of most other cultures, tend to be workaholics. If you've spent any time in a tropical or third world country, you'll know this to be true. Because, for many of these other cultures, the work ethic is to simply do what you must to *get by*, and then to relax and enjoy life the rest of the time. Note: this can be highly frustrating to your average, and somewhat uptight, American tourist.

But we could learn a thing or two from some of our more laid-back neighbors. Perhaps this is where the expression "less is more" originated. For many in these other cultures know how to get along with less money, less prestige, and less stress in order to gain more relaxation, more family-time, and more of the simple pleasures that make life worth living. Now, really, which culture is "more advanced?"

FOR FURTHER REFLECTION

Pause to consider that you live in a very work-oriented society. But this isn't the way all the world thinks. Accept that there are many things we can learn from other cultures—that we, Americans, don't know it all. Invite God to give you His "work ethic."

PRAYER

Gracious Father, I admit that I am greatly influenced by my culture. I invite You to help me to understand how You value my work and time. Teach me Your ways. Amen

What Really Matters

For with you is the fountain of life; in your light we see light.
—Psalm 36:9

If someone gets knocked down with a debilitating illness, they quickly begin to understand what really matters in life. Suddenly, they may realize what consumed them yesterday was only shallow, superfluous, or insignificant. Because of their new and unstable circumstances, their values have drastically shifted.

But do we really need to fear for our life before we can figure out what *really* matters? Isn't that what we're working toward as we seek to eliminate stress and anxiety—to replace those ill feelings with a focus on what's truly important and significant in our lives? Because it's inevitable, the time will come for each of us to give an account for our lives. How much better if we begin to understand what really matters right now!

FOR FURTHER REFLECTION

What is it that really matters to you? Do you live life with those things in mind? How much time and energy do you invest in what really matters? Is there room to make some changes? Ask God to lead you.

PRAYER

Loving Creator, will I ever figure this out? Please, help me to invest my best energies into the parts of my life that really matter. Please, remind me when I neglect them. Amen

Relationship Evaluation

Come near to God and he will come near to you.

—James 4:8

Throughout our lives, we are surrounded by a continuum of relationships. In our families, in our neighborhoods, at work, from our past, in our future . . . they just keep coming and going. And sometimes we take them for granted—taking both the good and the bad in stride. But would it be wise to become more intentional in our relationships?

As we evaluate how we invest our time and energy, we may, likewise, want to evaluate the relationships we invest ourselves in. We have only so much time and energy to spend, and healthy relationships are vital to our well-being. But if we invest ourselves in the wrong people, we'll eventually pay the price. We find ourselves pulled in different, and often frustrating, directions. But if we understand our friendships, and prioritize them accordingly, we can invest the quality time that's needed to nurture a good relationship. And the blessing will be twofold!

FOR FURTHER REFLECTION

Consider who you've spent most of your time with lately. Is this someone you consider a "best" friend? Someone who's true to you, loyal to you, has your best interests at heart? If not, ask yourself why. Then show your best friend how much you appreciate him or her.

PRAYER

Dear Jesus, help me to be a good, loyal, dependable friend. Remind me that You're the best "best friend" I'll ever have. Amen

Running the Good Race

However, I consider my life worth nothing to me, if only I may finish the race and complete the task the Lord Jesus has given me—the task of testifying to the gospel of God's grace.

—Acts 20:24

With so much focus on slowing down, why would we want to consider a "race" metaphor just now? Because when we're trying to make changes in our lives, it can sometimes feel like a workout or "race" of sorts. So, let's consider marathon runners and how they prepare for an endurance race. Let's see how it compares with our lives.

First of all, they meticulously guard the health of their bodies—they eat nutritiously, get plenty of rest, drink lots of water, get check-ups, buy the correct running shoes. Next, they warm up and exercise, keeping their muscles in shape. And finally, they run daily, no excuses (come rain or shine). In other words, they're running the good race every single day. They know if they don't stay the course of daily training that they'll never be able to seriously compete in the actual marathon. Just like life.

FOR FURTHER REFLECTION

Consider the daily disciplines it takes to keep your stress levels down: simple things like eating right, sleeping well, praying, and thinking happy thoughts. Are you neglecting anything? Decide, for your benefit, to get yourself back on track today.

PRAYER

Remind me, God, that I'm running the "good race" every day. Help me to stay on track in all areas of my life. Thank you for coaching me through the tough times. Amen

Smell the Roses

Let my teaching fall like rain and my words descend like dew,
like showers on new grass, like abundant rain on tender plants.
—Deuteronomy 32:2

How often do we need to be reminded to "stop and smell the roses" before we actually get the message and do it automatically? For those of us who are trying to emerge from the stress zone, it might take awhile. But, hopefully, the time will come when we're doing it without thinking, and others will wonder how we ever got there.

So, let's remember to take time to really listen to the ones we love, to drive more slowly, to sing out loud, to breathe deeply, to remember someone who's gone, to praise God, to smell something good in the air, to dream dreams, to look at old photos, to celebrate past successes, to light a candle, to take a stroll. So many things, if we could only take the time.

FOR FURTHER REFLECTION

Decide today that you'll do something you haven't done in ages. This might require some real thinking. Then allow yourself the time to do it, extricating yourself from previous commitments if you have to, and scheduling this activity into your day. Make sure you do it—and then try to do it spontaneously next time.

PRAYER

Eternal God, I know I must be missing out on things each day.
Please help me to understand the importance of "small" pleasures.
Show me how to enjoy them. Amen

Pressure from Within

Out of the same mouth come praise and cursing. My brothers,
this should not be. Can both fresh water and salt water flow
from the same spring?

—James 3:10, 11

We face lots of external pressure each day, most of which we can do little or nothing about—other than learn to not be unraveled by it. But we need to remember that a fair amount of pressure still comes from within. And although we've made real progress in this area, some old, ingrained ways may still remain—ways of thinking, acting, and speaking that we're accustomed to, and may not even notice.

Some of these pressures within us are simply remnants from childhood. Old and erroneous lessons we learned about not measuring up, not performing well enough, not making the grade. And so we might silently (and sometimes not so silently) berate ourselves, chastising ourselves in the same way a teacher once did in grade school. But it's time to quit. We need to check these thoughts and words at the door and replace them with positive ones that energize and revive us, like water from a cool, clear spring.

FOR FURTHER REFLECTION

Listen to the words you speak to yourself throughout the day. Are these the words a good friend would say to you? The words your Father in heaven would speak to you? Decide to sift and toss away the words that are harmful. Replace them with words that are helpful.

PRAYER

Heavenly father, help me to recognize when I'm being too hard on myself. I want to hear the words You would speak to me. Help me to think more positively about myself. Amen

New Each Morning

Because of the Lord's great love we are not consumed,
for his compassions never fail. They are new every morning;
great is your faithfulness.

—Lamentations 3:22, 23

What if every single morning we could rise and shine, with happy hearts, knowing that our life's slate has been cleaned and cleared, and that we're now ready for a brand new, fresh, and unsoiled day? Wouldn't it be great? *Well, we can!*

Because God's gracious and cleansing forgiveness for us is as fresh and pure as the new day—and it never stops flowing. And because of His mercy, we *can* rise up and know that nothing we did yesterday will be held against us today. Not in God's eyes anyway. And isn't that what matters most?

But all this mercy is worthless if we don't believe God, embrace Him, and receive it. For what use is His forgiveness if we refuse to accept it? So, each morning, let's remember that God has forgiven us, and let's forgive ourselves too!

FOR FURTHER REFLECTION

Remind yourself that God, through His son Jesus Christ, has forgiven us everything— past, present, future. And that all we must do is believe Him and receive it. Then rejoice that your slate's been wiped clean, and a fresh new day awaits you!

PRAYER

Dear God, Thank You for forgiving me.
Help me to remember that Your forgiveness is constant and daily.
Help me to celebrate Your mercies each morning! Amen

The Task at Hand

Whatever you do, work at it with all your heart,
as working for the Lord, not for men.

—Colossians 3:23

One of the easiest ways to become totally overwhelmed is to mentally run through every single little thing that you think you must accomplish—in a day, a week, a year, your entire life. Whew! Talk about an overload of stress-inducing heartburn! But we don't have to live like that. Instead, how about if we train ourselves to focus on the task at hand?

For instance, when we're driving we could focus on doing it safely and well. When we're fixing food, we could do it to our best ability. When we're on the job, we could work as if God were our boss. By learning to focus on the task at hand, we train our minds to block out other unnecessary stress factors that might try to distract us. And it keeps us calm and peaceful. Not only that, but we do a much better job too.

FOR FURTHER REFLECTION

Whenever possible, try to think in a more single-minded manner, training your mind to focus on only what you're doing, and blocking out all unnecessary distractions. Direct your energy into the task at hand. Enjoy the satisfaction of work well done.

PRAYER

Dear Lord, help me to focus on whatever it is I'm doing,
and to do it with my best intelligence and energy.
Help me to work and live, mindful that You are watching. Amen

Alive and Well?

Keep alert, stand firm in your faith, be courageous, be strong.
—1 Corinthians 16:13

So, we're moving along gracefully now. We're learning to say "no." We're getting our priorities straight. Life's pace feels a little more comfortable, things are almost under control. Or, if not, at least we can see the light at the end of the tunnel. And for all practical purposes we're alive and well and doing, we think, pretty good.

But that's probably the time we need to be on our guard. For just as we think things are getting better, going smoothly, we might be tempted to take on something new—a challenge perhaps—but it might be something that will knock us off balance. So, instead of giving into something that might not be for our best, why not use this time for a little R&R? Why not just put our feet up for a moment and enjoy a little rest; or go outside and enjoy some recreation? Just because the water seems smooth doesn't mean we should rock the boat.

FOR FURTHER REFLECTION

Take a moment to rejoice at the progress you are making. But don't let it go to your head. You still need to guard yourself. Get in the habit of enjoying "down" time. Allow yourself to just hang with the ones you love. Refresh yourself. It's okay to take it easy.

PRAYER

Please, God, remind me again of where I've been and where I'm going. Don't let me overload my plate again. Help me to hear Your voice as You guide me safely along. Amen

We Are Not Perfect

*Yet, O Lord, you are our Father. We are the clay, you are the
potter; we are all the work of your hand.*

—Isaiah 64:8

We really do know we're not perfect—at least in most parts of our
brains. But a few small cracks or crevices may remain that aren't
completely convinced of our imperfect nature. And it's entirely
possible that we might still get rather disappointed when we fail.
And we *do* fail, don't we? Sometimes miserably. But we need to
accept that it's just part of our human condition, then rise back
up, dust ourselves off, ask God to forgive us and help us, and then
continue onward.

Because our imperfections shouldn't overwhelm us anymore
than the fact that we cannot (without the aid of aircraft) fly. It's
just not the way God made us. In fact, it's quite likely He made us
with all these human imperfections just so we'd be continually
reminded of how much we need Him to make it through this life.
And He never tires of us coming to Him for help. In fact, He
delights in it!

FOR FURTHER REFLECTION

*Once again, admit that you're not perfect—never will be. In fact,
decide that you can rejoice in it. Know that your imperfections are
what draw you near to God. And then remember that He's the One
who made you like He did—and God makes no mistakes!*

PRAYER

*Thank You, Lord, for making me with all these human imperfections.
And if I get better, I'll know it's because of You.
Please, change me into what pleases You. Amen*

It's Okay to Decline

The mind of the wise makes their speech judicious,
and adds persuasiveness to their lips.

—Proverbs 16:23

We've already talked about saying "no." And hopefully we're all learning to incorporate that powerful little word into our vocabularies. But perhaps it's time for a refresher and expansion course. It's also okay to decline what can seem like a good opportunity. Have you ever noticed how you can get caught up in something like that? Perhaps it's something you've longed for: a promotion at work, a position in the community, a personal advancement . . . and it just seems *too good to pass up.*

And maybe it is. Or maybe it's not. Before you accept, give it careful and prayerful thought. Just because it looks good doesn't mean it's good *for you.* Wisely estimate the amount of additional time and energy this could require, and ask yourself if you (your relationships, your sanity, etc.) can afford it. Then answer honestly.

FOR FURTHER REFLECTION

Perhaps there isn't a big opportunity knocking on your door today, but be aware that one could knock at anytime. Decide today that if this happens (whether big or small) you will consider it with wisdom and surround it with prayer. Determine to make wise life-decisions always.

PRAYER

Dear Jesus, help me to be mindful that all "good" opportunities aren't necessarily good for me. Teach me to be wise and discerning, and to come to You for direction. Amen

One Eye on Eternity

I know that whatever God does endures forever;
nothing can be added to it, nor anything taken from it;
God has done this, so that all should stand in awe before him.
                                                    —Ecclesiastes 3:14

One of the best dividends of simplifying our lives, getting our perspectives straight, and allowing God to lead us, is that it helps us to see the bigger picture more clearly. We begin to realize and respect that our earthly lives are only a small, although highly important, part of our existence. But we begin to understand that God has a much bigger plan. An eternal plan—and it seems that the best is yet to come!

And so, living a more calm, peaceful, and controlled life, we begin to learn how to keep one eye on eternity as we proceed along. We begin to recognize opportunities to tell others about where we're going, and where we've been. We begin to understand that there's more to life than meets the eye. And we actually have time to ponder these things!

FOR FURTHER REFLECTION

Take some time today to consider what eternity means to you. Does it make you uneasy? Or do you look forward to it? Does it seem like you're already participating in eternity, right here on earth? Does your link with God assure you that eternity is real?

PRAYER

Almighty God, only You fully comprehend the depth and dimension of eternity. But I'd like to know a little more about it. Please, help me to understand it better. Amen

Seize the Day!

This is the day that the Lord has made;
let us rejoice and be glad in it.

—Psalm 118:24

What a glorious wonder today is! Do we really appreciate that there will never be another one exactly like it? Do we ask ourselves how we can honor God for this magnificent gift? Is there some way He can use us in some amazing new way today? In other words, how can we seize the day?

For as we progress toward a life that's more directed, more fulfilling—not to mention less stressful and fraught with difficulty—we begin to realize how we have more energy, more positive emotion, more delight and real enthusiasm. And, we begin to recognize how it's truly possible to seize the day. So, what is it that we want to do today? And how can we do it with heartfelt gusto and joyful eagerness? Let's do it! Let's seize the day!

FOR FURTHER REFLECTION

Make this a day to rejoice. Celebrate your victories and praise God for the way He has led you. Then make it a special time, do something out of the ordinary, and seize the day!

PRAYER

Gracious God, I praise You for what You're doing in my life. Show me something great that I can do today. Help me to rejoice in every new day, and to thank You for each one. Amen

Reaching Out

*I pray that the sharing of your faith may become effective
when you perceive all the good that we may do for Christ.*

—Philemon 1:6

We might remember a time in our lives, perhaps not so very long ago, when the mere idea of reaching out to help another seemed completely overwhelming. Perhaps it's because our own lives were so immersed in stress and anxiety that the very thought of helping someone else felt a little like a non-swimmer trying to rescue someone who was drowning. It looked hopeless, and we feared we'd both go under.

But perhaps that's changed (or is changing) and suddenly we're feeling more empowered and capable, even eager, to reach out to help someone else. And what a healthy place that is, and what a gift to be able to encourage another. So, let's be aware of any in need that God has placed around us. Perhaps there's someone nearby who needs a helping hand, an uplifting word. Let's ask God to use us in the life of another.

FOR FURTHER REFLECTION

Do you feel ready to reach out to someone else today, even in a small and seemingly insignificant way? If so, take a moment to ask God to lead you, and then be on the lookout for someone who may be in need. Then enjoy the satisfaction of reaching out—satisfaction born of your sincere and God-inspired desire to help, rather than old and harmful "need to please" habits.

PRAYER

Loving Father, I know You desire that Your children reach out to one another. Please, strengthen me, and show me someone You'd like to help and bless through me. Help me to do this without slipping into the harmful habits I once had. Amen

God's Covenant

Never again will the waters become a flood to destroy all life.
—Genesis 9:15

God promised it. We believe it. And we can live what we believe. We've been building a sturdy sandbag wall to stave off the floodwaters of chaos, anxiety, and over-scheduling, and we know that wall, with God's help, will hold. We've been enlightened to the destructive toll stress can take on us physically, emotionally, and spiritually and we have resolved to respect ourselves, and to honor God's glorious gift to us—the gift of life—by refusing to allow tension, pressure, and strain to steal our joy.

Just as we will always have challenges and difficulties, we will always have God's promise that He will be there to save us. He will keep us afloat. When we feel overwhelmed by threats—real or imagined—to our well-being, we can find calming strength in His blessed assurance that we are safe in His arms. And that certainly makes our burdens feel a whole lot lighter.

FOR FURTHER REFLECTION

Take a moment to recognize the life God has been building for you. Rejoice over the changes that have moved you toward a more ordered and peaceful place.

PRAYER

Dear God, thank You for leading me to a place of order and serenity. Help me to be wise and sensible, resisting the temptation to embrace activities that could break through my sandbag wall and steal my peace. Amen

Choosing Our Battles

Moses answered the people, "Do not be afraid. . . .
The Lord will fight for you; you need only to be still."
—Exodus 14:13, 14

Even as we enjoy a more controlled lifestyle, we cannot escape all of life's battles. And sometimes we must even go to war for the sake of peace. For instance, we must contend with the daily barrage of all that would come against us and dissuade us from our goal to live focused, intentional, and relatively stress-free lives. Pressures will continue to mount from all angles, trying to overwhelm us, and we must be armed against them.

On the other hand, some battles may be completely unnecessary. These unworthy battles are simply distractions that attempt to sap our strength and to engage us in areas where there is no reward, and where there may be negative consequences. We need to position ourselves so we won't be pulled into these skirmishes (whether at work or at home). We need to pray for wisdom to discern how to best spend our energy, time, and passion.

FOR FURTHER REFLECTION

Are you engaged in a battle that is draining and frustrating? Have you asked yourself if this is really a battle worth fighting? Or a battle you have been called to fight? Have you asked God to lead you and to fight for you? Take a moment to consider these things.

PRAYER

Dear Lord, help me to recognize when I'm involved
in a battle that You haven't called me to participate in.
Help me to use my energy wisely. Show me Your way. Amen

Be Prepared to Have Fun

So I commend the enjoyment of life, because nothing is better
for a man under the sun than to eat and drink and be glad.
—Ecclesiastes 8:15

Sometimes we are suddenly presented with an unexpected chunk
of free time. Perhaps an appointment is canceled; a little league
game is rained out; or someone kindly offers to watch the kids for
the day. But we're caught by surprise, and we're not quite sure how
to enjoy this time. As a result, we might waste an afternoon at the
mall, spending money we wish we hadn't for something we didn't
even want.

But before this happens, let's sit down and create a "fun list"
packed with all those things we want to do, but never seem to have
time for. Things like a trip to the library or local bookstore; or
visiting an old friend; or an uninterrupted roam through a
museum; or picking out fabric for that quilt we dream of making.
. . . Whatever it is, let's put it on the list. And then, even if an
unexpected time doesn't pop up, let's do our fun things anyway!
When we become aware of our desires we are far more likely to
take action.

FOR FURTHER REFLECTION

Begin compiling a list of all the things you wish you had time to do.
They can be big or small, requiring a short period of time or days.
But just start getting these ideas down on paper. Then save the list
and work your way down it—savoring every experience.

PRAYER

Thank You, God. You've created such an enjoyable world.
Remind me of the importance of taking time to experience it
more fully. Teach me to take the time for pleasure. Amen

Clear the Table

I will sprinkle clean water on you, and you will be clean; I will cleanse you from all your impurities and from all your idols.
—Ezekiel 36:25

It can be a daily challenge to remain stress-free. And sometimes, in the flash of a moment, we suddenly feel ourselves becoming overwhelmed all over again. But let's remember that that's normal—just like keeping the garden weed-free takes regular maintenance. Often it's the small things that get to us—small things that for some reason begin to feel large. Perhaps it's just an accumulation of junk mail splayed across the kitchen counter, or the clutter your husband just piled on the dining room table. And maybe we don't even realize it, but somehow these "little messes" make us feel totally stressed-out.

Well, it's time to simply clear out the clutter. Restore order. Show your world who's boss (at least in the areas where you can!). And once we feel ourselves regaining control and composure, those feelings of frustration and stress simply melt away.

FOR FURTHER REFLECTION

Remind yourself that you can conquer the clutter in your life. One step you can take to greatly reduce the amount of junk mail you receive is to send a self-addressed, stamped envelope to Mail Preference Service, Direct Marketing Association, P.O. Box 9008, Farmingdale, NY, 11735, with a note requesting a free "mail preference" registration form.

PRAYER

Almighty God, sometimes it's the small things that get me down. Help me to not be overwhelmed by the minutia in my life. Remind me that no problem is too big or too small for You to handle for me. Amen

Make a Play-Date

My guilt has overwhelmed me like a burden too heavy to bear.
—Psalm 38:4

We talked about making a "fun list" of all those things we want to do. But in addition to all of the other distractions in our lives, does guilt ever stop us from doing the things on our list? It bears repeating that God wants us to lead joyful lives. Yet many of us, especially those with type "A" personalities, or who are just barely escaping from a stressed-out workaholic lifestyle, seem to think we're not meant to have fun. Sure, other people have it, but it's just not ours for the asking. Well, it *is* ours for the asking, but it will never simply "just happen." We must *make* it happen and we must *allow* it to work for us when it does.

So maybe we need to completely change our way of thinking, and begin to accept how very vital playtime is. It's almost like a vaccination against disease, and it helps us function better in other areas of our lives. So let's schedule a play-date today!

FOR FURTHER REFLECTION

Consider how you "play." Be it a sport or a hobby or whatever you do just for the pure fun and pleasure of doing it, ask yourself if you ever allow some of that rare fun to be spoiled by feelings of guilt. Recognize that you are allowed to have fun and that you need to have a balance of work and play in your life.

PRAYER

Loving Creator, show me some good ways I can make playing a regular part of my life. And please help me to not feel guilty for it. Help me to keep my life balanced. Amen

No Limits to God's Love

Now there are varieties of gifts, but the same Spirit; and there are
varieties of services, but the same Lord; and there are varieties
of activities, but it is the same God who activates
all of them in everyone.

—1 Corinthians 12:4-6

One of the best ways to alleviate frustration is to understand and
accept that we are all given different gifts, and that we may not
shine in certain areas. So often we put unnecessary pressures on
ourselves, somehow imagining that we are expected to excel in all
disciplines. But that would be greedy. We need to let go of these
inflated expectations of ourselves. And we need to joyfully accept
our gifts, realizing that we are just as God made us, and that He
knows what He's doing in our lives. And as we accept these things,
we also experience newfound freedom in doing that which is
within our realm—and doing it well.

FOR FURTHER REFLECTION

Admit to yourself that you can't do it all. But realize that you don't
need to do it all, and that God made you just like you are for good
reason. Rejoice in it!

PRAYER

Eternal God, thank You for making me just the way You did.
Help me to fully understand what I am able to do, and to accept
what I may not be meant to do with gratitude and joy. Amen

Nurture Your Soul

You turned my wailing into dancing; you removed by sackcloth and clothed me with joy, that my heart may sing to you and not be silent. O Lord my God, I will give you thanks forever.
—Psalm 30:11, 12

We often neglect an inner part of our being. Call it our heart, our soul—it's that God-given part within us that holds our emotions and intellect. That part of us that appreciates an evocative painting, a moving song, or a beautiful line of prose. And sometimes we unwittingly starve or neglect that part of ourselves. We forget that attending an art exhibit changes us. We don't realize that listening to a symphony moves us. We fail to pick up a book that will communicate to a hidden place within us.

We forget to nurture our souls. And as a result the rest of our lives suffer a little. Sure, we might not notice, at first. Like someone who survives on fast food and never misses the pleasure of a gourmet meal—we might not miss what it is our soul is craving. But when we take the time to nurture our souls, we begin to understand and appreciate what a difference it can make in our lives.

FOR FURTHER REFLECTION

When was the last time you took in a concert or an exhibit or read a good book? Think for a moment about that which delights your soul. Is it a certain kind of music? Poetry? A walk in the woods? Whatever it is, decide to pursue it as a regular part of your life.

PRAYER

Father in heaven, thank You for creating me with a soul that needs to experience beauty. Show me ways to reconnect with my soul.
Amen

Eternal Optimists

For surely I know the plans I have for you, says the Lord, plans for your welfare and not for harm, to give you a future with hope.
—Jeremiah 29:11

Do you ever get the feeling that people think you actually *want* to run yourself ragged? That the only reason you're working till all hours of the night is that you enjoy it? That if you wanted to change you would? Well, it is up to us to set our minds to our new course—and stay on track. But we know it goes so much deeper than that, don't we?

First of all, we may feel forced to stay in an unhealthy situation by financial circumstances, or by an admirable sense of responsibility and loyalty. Or perhaps those of us who are overwhelmed tend to be among the most optimistic people around. Maybe we just plain believe that we can make a situation better; that things will always improve; that if we just keep on keepin' on things will turn around. Well, they will—but that doesn't mean we don't have to actively pursue that better situation, through prayer and vigilant dedication to hearing God's plan for us.

FOR FURTHER REFLECTION

Do you ever use your faith as an excuse to remain in an untenable position? Or to be taken advantage of? Remember that God wants the best for you, and be aware of how you might need to change some things in your life to let that happen.

PRAYER

Lord Jesus, I believe in You. I know You have saved me. Thank You for my faith and my optimism. Please help me to recognize when they may be preventing me from making necessary changes. Amen

The Truth Will Set You Free

The Lord is near to all who call on him,
to all who call on him in truth.

—Psalm 145:18

Don't we long for freedom? Living in a free country, we might consider ourselves to be fairly free—but are we really? And if we're not, have we considered what might be keeping us from experiencing real freedom? What we don't always realize is that living a less than honest life can be like living in a virtual prison. When we allow half-truths or falsehoods into our lives, we become trapped in a web that can be not only stressful, but totally debilitating. For instance, if we don't admit to our boss how crushed we're feeling by our workload, or to our spouse how put-upon we feel at home, how can we expect anything to change?

So, let's decide to embrace truth, and experience all the glorious freedom that comes with it. Let's ask God to create honest hearts within us, and to help us to speak the truth in love. And then, let's live freely and joyfully!

FOR FURTHER REFLECTION

Examine your heart—are integrity, honesty, and truth vitally important to you? Commit yourself to living honestly (both inwardly and outwardly). Ask God to help you recognize and deal with any less than truthful behaviors you may be exhibiting.

PRAYER

Dear God, I know You value honesty. And I admit I sometimes don't even know the depths of my own heart. Please, create a clean and truthful heart within me. And help me to reveal my truths to those around me, lovingly and respectfully. Amen

Finishing Strong

I have fought the good fight, I have finished the race,
I have kept the faith.

—2 Timothy 4:7

As we continue in this endurance race of life, we may occasionally need to be reminded to keep our eyes on the finish line. This can be a challenge since we usually don't know how long this race will be—one mile, five miles, a cross-country marathon? When our goal isn't in sight, we tend to just get caught up in the pace. We dash from deadline to deadline, and sprint from one activity to another, but we don't realize what we've been running past or what we're really running toward. We lose our focus, energy, and enthusiasm.

But if we remember that we have a reason for being here, that we are running this race for God, we can finish strong. No one wants to be that runner who hits the wall only midway through the race—or perhaps even worse, when the finish line is just within sight. We want to be those runners who deliberately pace ourselves, heed our Coach, and then run consistently and evenly until we cross the finish line and rejoice over a well-run race.

FOR FURTHER REFLECTION

Stop for a moment to consider what you're running toward and what shape you'll be in when you reach your goal. Remind yourself that God is an everlasting source of strength for the endurance race of life we are running. Ask yourself if you've been attuned to His guidance and wisdom.

PRAYER

Merciful God, give me strength. Help me to keep going in the face of whatever comes my way. Thank you for being with me always.
Amen

Change Is Good

I have set the Lord always before me.
Because he is at my right hand, I will not be shaken.

—Psalm 16:8

We may love the plans we've made, but more often than not something comes along and completely changes them. Change happens. It arrives in the form of an unexpected baby, an ailing parent, a sudden job transfer or layoff, or even a twisted ankle. It's just a part of life. And we need to not only accept inevitable change, but embrace it. For fighting against change will only invite further stress and frustration. Instead we need to ask what we can learn from it.

When we see change as an opportunity for growth rather than an annoyance thwarting our carefully constructed plans, we give God a chance to refine us. We are reminded that He is in control and will bring good out of what might at first appear to be bad.

FOR FURTHER REFLECTION

Consider your attitude toward change. Do you usually fight and resist it? Realize that only as you accept change as a healthy and normal part of life can you be free from the anxiety and dread that come from not knowing what's around the next corner.

PRAYER

Help me, God, to trust You more. Help me to believe You have a good plan for my life—one that inevitably involves changes of some kind. Teach me to embrace them. Amen

Investing in Others

So the Lord spoke kind and comforting words to the angel
who talked with me.

—Zechariah 1:13

We're surrounded by all sorts of investment opportunities—through work-related benefits, online brokers, stocks and bonds. . . . Yet often these types of financial risks can bring a stress all their own, with no guarantee of a return on our investment. But there's another kind of investment, one that is not without an element of stress occasionally, but nonetheless can fortify our spirits in ways that sustain us through the daily and often overwhelming frustrations and pressures associated with living.

And that is to invest in others. Be a friend; have a friend. Having a close companion—whether family, friend, or coworker—to share the turmoil as well as the peace (when we manage to find it!) in our lives can mean the difference between cracking under the weight of life and rising above it.

FOR FURTHER REFLECTION

Prayerfully consider the kind of sincere companionship you can offer—without compromising your emotional and physical peace. Remember that there is a give and take to all personal relationships, but that neither one of you is supposed to be the only one giving.

PRAYER

Gracious Father, thank You for the friends you've given me.
Show me the kind of friend You would like me to be.
Direct my energies in paths that will honor and glorify You. Amen

True Riches

But strive for the greater gifts. And I will show you
a still more excellent way.

—1 Corinthians 12:31

When we consider ways to invest in others, it's also a good time to reevaluate what it is that truly makes us rich. And although we tend to think in terms of salary, savings accounts, and home equity, we need to remember that the time will eventually come when all earthly wealth will be worthless to us. We need to realize that one day we will stand before God with nothing in our hands but our hearts.

And when we truly understand these things, we'll begin to keep our daily lives in perspective—and in turn find deep peace. For we will no longer feel the compulsion to strive and compete for our temporary treasure. Instead, we might focus our energy on the kinds of treasure that last forever—things like love, faith, mercy, kindness, peace . . . and we might also discover those eternal treasures to be of infinite value right here on earth!

FOR FURTHER REFLECTION

Think about what is most valuable to you. Be honest. Do you place great value upon things—cars, homes, furnishings, clothes, stuff? Is this a distraction to what you know is really more important? Like relationships, living in peace, reaching out to others?

PRAYER

Ever-present God, help me to understand what is really valuable in this life. Help me to focus my time and energy on the riches that will last forever. Please, lead me. Amen

A Spirit-Led Life

And see, I am sending upon you what my Father promised;
so stay here in the city until you have been clothed
with power from on high.

—Luke 24:49

Sometimes our desire to live a life that pleases and honors God can feel overwhelming. We wonder how we can possibly accomplish this thing. How we can live without disappointing God. It's too difficult—we'd have to be perfect to keep from failing. But I suspect God knew we'd feel this way. Perhaps that's why He is completely available to pick up all of us weak and struggling humans, unable to make it on our own, and sustain us.

When we plead for help, God has promised to put His Spirit within us, to lead and guide and teach us how to live. All we must do is ask. And with His Spirit in us, we begin to experience new power that helps us face our challenges—victoriously!

FOR FURTHER REFLECTION

Consider whether God's Spirit dwells within you. Have you asked Him to come into your heart? To rule and to reign there? To lead and to guide you every single day of your life? Invite God to participate in your life with a new level of commitment and intimacy.

PRAYER

Precious Lord, I invite You to live within me
through the power and presence of Your Spirit.
I long for this close connection with You. Amen

"Final" Mission Statement

The Lord your God has blessed you in all the work of your hands.
He has watched over your journey through this vast desert.
—Deuteronomy 2:7

We probably will never really have a "final" mission statement. Because just as our lives are constantly evolving and changing, we want to remain able to adapt our focus and goals as God leads and directs us. But for the sake of this book, let's take one "last" look at our mission statement. Let's evaluate whether or not it seems to be truly directed in the way we want to go. And let's pray that God will help us to develop it more fully over time.

Perhaps we want to hone it down to three or four short sentences. Each sentence should convey a clear sense of what our life's priorities are (at least as we see them today). Things like a commitment to keep God first in our lives; to cherish our loved ones; to reach out on the job or in the community; or, because we don't want to forget about including ourselves in our statement, perhaps a line related to a dream we'd like to pursue.

FOR FURTHER REFLECTION

Look over your mission statement and determine whether or not it could use some refining. Try to streamline it. Keep the wording as simple and concise as possible. Make sure your priorities are clear. Invite, once again, God's direction.

PRAYER

Dear God, I bring my mission statement before you, asking that You help me to compose it in a way that honors You. For You know the way I should go. Amen

Pass It On

Therefore encourage one another and build each other up,
just as in fact you are doing.

—1 Thessalonians 5:11

As we progress in life, conquering challenges, restoring order, living a life that feels controlled and directed and hopeful—we can't help but want to share where we've been, and where we're now heading, with others. Especially those who seem to be experiencing some of the same troubles that we are leaving behind. It's a pleasure to be able to give good directions to someone who's lost their way when you've recently found the right road yourself.

And people are often more inclined to listen to someone "who's been there"—someone who's emerged from a challenge with knowledge and experience—not to mention some notable outward changes. So let's enjoy sharing what we've faced and how we are conquering. And let's take someone's hand and encourage them along the road we're traveling. For it's such a joy when we go together!

FOR FURTHER REFLECTION

Is there someone you know who seems overwhelmed by the pressures of their life? Do you feel an inner nudging to reach out to them with a word of encouragement? Ask God to lead you, then be willing to take the next step.

PRAYER

Please, Lord, show me if there's someone who needs
my advice or encouragement. Then help me to approach them
with a humble heart of kindness and love. Amen

Sleeping Like a Baby

You will keep in perfect peace him whose mind is steadfast,
because he trusts in you.

—Isaiah 26:3

We sometimes long for that deep sort of rest—that kind where we totally relax and just *sleep like a baby*. Consider how newborns sleep: with no worries, no cares, no anxiety, no fear. They simply sleep with the blessed assurance that every need will be met by their loving caretaker, who has nothing but their very best interests at heart.

But isn't that how it is with God? Doesn't He have our very best interests at heart, too? If we really believe that, and we truly trust Him, shouldn't we also be able to simply let go and rest like that—to *sleep like a baby*? So, perhaps we should imagine ourselves as His dear little children, loved unconditionally, nestled safe and snug in His strong arms, as we too relax completely and drift off into that sweet and blissful rest.

FOR FURTHER REFLECTION

Consider your ability to trust God. Are you able to lay all your worries and cares at His feet, and to believe that He will see you through? Tonight, before you go to sleep, envision yourself as His little child, safe in His arms, and try to sleep like a baby.

PRAYER

Gentle Lord, I want that childlike faith that trusts You implicitly with all areas of my life. Please, teach me to trust You more, and help me rest in You. Amen

No Clock in Heaven

With the Lord a day is like a thousand years,
and a thousand years are like a day.

—2 Peter 3:8

Eternity is a lot for the human mind to fathom. How can we begin to wrap our minds around the concept of "forever"? Perhaps we begin by realizing that there are no clocks in heaven. Time, as we know it, will cease to exist. Perhaps there will be another dimension for measuring. Perhaps not. But we can be assured that we'll no longer worry about being late. We'll no longer grow anxious over time that's steadily ticking away.

But maybe we can begin enjoying a little eternity now. Maybe we can train ourselves to not be so addicted to our timepieces. But to enjoy the moments that God gives us, living each day to the best of our ability, and not fretting over someone who's a few minutes late, or berating ourselves for not moving fast enough. For, if we truly believe in eternity, we have all the time in the world. So, what's the rush?

FOR FURTHER REFLECTION

Remind yourself that you are already walking in eternity. Then take a deep breath and simply relax. Try not to be ruled by the clock today. In fact, if you normally wear a wristwatch, go without it. Instead, invite God to lead and guide you and show you what's really important.

PRAYER

Eternal God, help me to have just a tiny glimpse of the way you view time. Remind me that You have all the time in the world and that forever is a long, long time. Amen

The Greatest Is Love

And now these three remain: faith, hope and love.
But the greatest of these is love.

—1 Corinthians 13:13

As we simplify our lives, eliminating those distractions that cause stress and pressure and anxiety, we subsequently enhance our ability to focus on other things. Hopefully, things of much greater value. It's likely we'll experience a heightened awareness of what's truly important; what makes life really worth living; and what we hope to achieve within our lifetimes.

And perhaps all this could be boiled down to one simple, and lasting, element: *Love.* For when love becomes the true center of our lives—love for God, love for others, love for ourselves—everything else seems to fall neatly into place. Decisions become simple. Priorities are established. The challenges in life no longer overwhelm us. Because we are ruled by love. And love's pure light illuminates our way.

FOR FURTHER REFLECTION

Read 1 Corinthians 13 (the chapter about love) and consider the many attributes of love. Then consider whether or not you are allowing love to rule your life. Ask God to help you to understand what love really is, and to help you grow in your capacity to love.

PRAYER

Merciful Lord, You are the God of love. And I long to be deeply rooted in Your love. Teach me to understand the attributes of love. Help me to begin by loving You more! Amen

Well Done!

As soon as all the people saw Jesus, they were overwhelmed with
wonder and ran to greet him.

—Mark 9:15

Sometimes being overwhelmed is a good thing. That is, when we are overwhelmed with wonder and awe and delight. One day, we expect to stand before our Heavenly Father, and we hope to see His beautiful smiling face—brighter than the midday sun. And, hopefully, we've done our best to live according to His plan and His purpose for us during our time on earth. Hopefully, we've served and obeyed Him with happy hearts of love—not perfectly, but with good intent. Hopefully, we've accepted His forgiveness and mercy—new every morning! And, hopefully, as a result of our effort and God's tender mercies, we've been loving and gracious and kind to those around us.

And on that glorious day, we hope that God will say, "Well done, My good and faithful servant!" And with joy we will then enter into His incredible kingdom, to celebrate His magnificent glory and His blessed presence throughout all eternity!

FOR FURTHER REFLECTION

Take a moment to imagine what heaven will be like. Envision God, Himself, greeting you and welcoming you in. Then remember that no matter how well we live our lives—it is only by God's amazing grace that we can enter into His kingdom.

PRAYER

Loving Father, once again, I receive your merciful forgiveness,
shown through Your Son, and I pray, when I see Your face,
You will be pleased with me, Your loving servant. Amen

Notes

Notes

Notes

Notes

Notes

Notes

Notes

Notes

Notes

Notes

Notes

Notes

Notes

Notes

Notes

Notes

Notes

Notes